Secret Greenh

Are you prepared for the next big disaster? How will you heat your home and your hot water? How will you grow food for your family year round? How do you keep others from taking it?

How to Build the Ultimate Homestead & Prepper Greenhouse

Rick Austin

The Survivalist Gardener

ISBN:1494417103
ISBN-13:9781494417109

DEDICATION

This book is dedicated to all those people, everywhere, who wish to take responsibility for their own welfare, and for the welfare of their families. Whether you call yourself a homesteader, a "prepper" a survivalist or something else, this book will help those of you who wish to be self-sufficient, to be able to provide an abundant supply of good healthy food for yourself and your family, in good times and in bad.

CONTENTS

ACKNOWLEDGMENTS

The last thing I wrote after this book was complete, is this standard obligatory section, that most people don't honestly read, where I am supposed to acknowledge who helped make this book possible, as well as which experts and people who have helped along the way. So here is an incomplete accounting of the people I would like to acknowledge, without whom, this book would have never been written.

First, I acknowledge my Dad who instilled in me at an early age the tenets of self-reliance, an appreciation for solar energy, plumbing, heating, and basic carpentry, and the knowledge of how to use tools, all of which have served me well over the years in my efforts to "MacGyver" just about everything. He also taught me that although there were many ways to run a pipe, (his way and every other way), that doing it right the first time, *always* saved money, time and frustration.

I acknowledge my friend Tim Will who many years ago turned me on to the premise of permaculture, which right then and there smacked me upside the head with the understanding that nature has been growing things quite successfully for millions of years, without man's help.

I acknowledge my friend Ron Hoover, of Plant Wise Solutions in Spindale, NC, who knows more about plants and what they need than I could ever learn in this lifetime;

I acknowledge my wife, who puts up with my "visionary projects" even though there is a lot of mud and dust between here and their completion;

I acknowledge my lifetime friend Merlin, who was a guardian angel in life and who I am sure, still is in death;

I acknowledge Survivor Jane, who taught me more about Social Media than I will ever know;

I acknowledge little Justine, who came into my life and taught me that no matter how old and fat you get, you can always be a kid at heart;

And I acknowledge our forefathers and the founders of this great country called The United States of America, where true personal freedom was established, and where men (and women) were once allowed to speak freely, be self-reliant, enterprising, and take care of their families...
May it not be destroyed by idiots.

CHAPTER-1
WHAT DO I KNOW?

Secret Garden of Survival has become the #1 Best Selling Book in Garden Design.

People that have read my book *Secret Garden of Survival-How to Grow a Camouflaged Food Forest* know that I have developed a system of agriculture that I call "NatureCulture™" where you create a food forest garden that lets nature do what it has been doing for millions of years; where there are symbiotic relationships between plants, with a series of mini eco-systems that also creates a garden which grows in 3 dimensions (as opposed to a traditional vegetable garden). The results of which have been nothing short of phenomenal.

The benefits of the *Secret Garden of Survival* are that you only have to plant once in your life-time, it takes very little space, grows 5x more food per square foot than a traditional garden, provides food for the next 30 years, and you never have to weed, never have to use fertilizers, and never have to use pesticide-- ever. And the whole garden is disguised to look like overgrown underbrush- so no one knows there is food growing there!

We went from red clay to a lush food forest in just two years.

The book was originally written as a survival garden book for "preppers" and for people who wanted to be self-sufficient homesteaders, but something unexpected happened "on the way to the forum".

The *Secret Garden of Survival* became the #1 Best Selling book in Garden Design in less than 10 months on the market. Not the #1 best-selling *survival garden book*- but the #1 book best-selling book in *all* garden design. That fact still floors me.

Those that know me, also know that I have been a so called "survivalist", "prepper" and self- sustainable homesteader for over 30 years. I have learned a few things along the way, and what I have learned, I have tried to incorporate into new buildings, and into each new property and homestead that I have built.

A couple of years ago, I wanted to build a greenhouse on my homestead that would incorporate many of the things I have learned about solar heating, insulation, growing plants, and self-sufficiency.

Of course, I wanted to be able to grow food year round, but I also knew that any greenhouse would have to fit into my gardening and homestead principles.

In other words, any greenhouse that I built would have to be sustainable, provide year round food, but also not use pesticides, not use fertilizers, allow for symbiotic/ companion planting, and it would have to fit with my prepper mentality. By prepper mentality, I mean it would have to be sustainable without electricity, have to be secure from marauders, and would have to be camouflaged (or hide in plain sight) so that people would not realize it was a source of food in the first place.

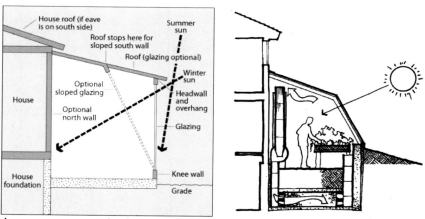

A sun room attached to a home can save on heating bills.

I also wanted my greenhouse to do far more than grow food. I knew from past research that a sun room attached to a home, could save on heating bills for the entire home if constructed properly. It could also collect and store solar heat if it had sufficient thermal mass, and it could act as a giant breadbox water heater for preheating water for the home.

According to Energy.gov, today the typical residential household in America uses 45% of its energy consumption just to heat the home, and another 18% of its energy consumption is typically used for heating hot water. Knowing this, then the best strategy in creating a sustainable home, is to reduce energy consumption of these two areas (that represent 63% of your energy usage)– first!

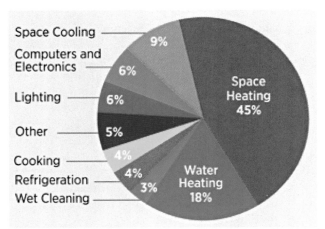

Space Cooling — 9%
Computers and Electronics — 6%
Lighting — 6%
Other — 5%
Cooking — 4%
Refrigeration — 4%
Wet Cleaning — 3%
Space Heating 45%
Water Heating 18%

63% of household energy consumption is for heating and hot water.

Thus, I wanted to be able to use the sun to heat the greenhouse and to store thermal energy, not only so that I could grow food year round, but also so that I could use the excess heat to heat my home. By the same token, I also wanted to be able to use the sun's energy to heat my hot water.

According to EnergyStar.gov, the typical US home consumes $2200.00 in energy per year. Potentially cutting that use by 63% for heating and hot water gives you a savings of about $1400.00 per year. (Thus reducing your electric bill from $2200.00 per year down to $800.00 per year!)

So accomplishing these two things alone, were well worth the time and cost of building the greenhouse, since the savings in energy, more than paid for its costs. Plus the knowledge that our home would be warm, even if there were no grid, was worth peace of mind that you just can't buy.

And having the ability to make hot water in a grid down scenario has huge benefits. Aside from daily personal hygiene which can keep your entire family healthier, hot water allows you to clean and disinfecting dishes, and clothing. And the psychological benefits of having a warm shower vs. cold showers, can have a dramatic positive effect on you and your group.

Clothes drying in the *Secret Greenhouse of Survival*.

Since washers and dryers consume another 6-10% of the typical home's energy bill, you can further reduce your power bill and make your homestead more sustainable, by using this greenhouse as a "clothes dryer".

By simply hanging up clothes to dry inside your greenhouse, you can let the sun do the work (the way your grandmother used to do on an outdoor clothes line) without collecting bird droppings, or having your bloomers on display for the neighbors to see. And as a prepper, this gives you more security (you don't have to go outside to hang your laundry) and you won't be showing hungry people, that there are souls living in your home.

But what type of greenhouse fits the bill for all these objectives?

One of the least expensive options for a greenhouse is a "hoop house". A hoop house is made out of bending PVC pipes in an arc to create a semi-circle frame (thus the "hoops"), along with plastic sheeting to cover the entire structure.

In a hoop house you must grow plants in beds, or in pots on the ground. Because of the semi-circle design, any tall plants have to be in pots in the center, which is exactly where you need to walk, because it is the only place with headroom. This limitation in its design means the you need to have a much longer building to grow an equivalent number of plants that you can grow in the *Secret Greenhouse of Survival.*

The design also means that you have to crawl on your hands and knees to reach plants near the sides of the frame where you cannot walk.

Also a hoop house won't last for the long haul, because over time the plastic sheeting will deteriorate from the sun, and it will rip in the cold, wind, and bad weather. (And where are you going to get more plastic sheeting when there are no more stores to buy it from?)

A hoop house is also not freeze proof. There is no thermal mass to store heat from the sun during the day, and although the less-than-paper-thin plastic covering is great for letting sun and heat in during the day, it also allows heat to escape (just as fast) at night. So unless you have a source of heat within the hoop house to keep it warm when it is below freezing outdoors, you are going to lose any plants that you have growing in there, when night falls and so does the temperature inside your hoop house.

Furthermore, needing a source of heat to keep a hoop house warm at night assumes that you can afford the energy bill to heat a totally inefficient building design, or that there will even be the ability to get that energy in grid down situation.

So a hoop house cannot be used year round to grow plants in any environment where your temperatures can go below freezing.

And, a hoop house is certainly not a secure place to grow your life or death food supply, at any time of the year, because anyone can cut through the plastic with a knife (or sharp claws) to steal your food. Thus hungry passersby as well as raccoons will be happy that you chose a plastic covered hoop house to grow your food.

The greenhouse pictured above is most certainly a beautiful building design and has a thermal mass of stone work around the bottom that collects heat from the sun during the day and gives off heat at night.

The height of the side windows allows for more freedom of movement within the greenhouse, as well as growing taller plants and potentially growing in 3 dimensions within the greenhouse.

But being almost entirely made of glass, it may be too hot in the summer time, and possibly too cold in the winter evenings, given that there is no insulation.

Of course, the thermal glass, certainly retains more heat than a hoop house, however, the size and shape of the tempered curved glass and/or plexi-glass panels tend to make them extremely expensive to start with, and even more expensive to replace.

And you may never be able to replace these glass panels in a grid down scenario, should a tree limb come falling down due to a storm, or should someone heave a rock through your windows, or just shoot a bullet through your greenhouse.

Of course, building this beautiful greenhouse is not a DYI (Do It Yourself) project either, given the complexity of the metal framing, the lifting of the heavy glass panels into place, and the overall construction involved in erecting this structure.

Aside from it being a hugely expensive, albeit beautiful building, it is also quite obviously a greenhouse, which makes you and your home a target for marauders, or just hungry passersby, should we have a Doomsday scenario (or even a short term loss of the rule of law), where a natural disaster occurs and the grocery stores are empty for a week or more.

And being all glass, should that situation happen, it is pretty much indefensible, and you are too, when you are in it.

This is the ultimate homestead greenhouse, but doesn't look like it.

Now, imagine a greenhouse that heats your home in the winter; heats your water; grows 5x more food /sq. ft. than a hoop house; provides food for you and your family all year long; can grow exotic foods (i.e. citrus in New England); allows you to start seedlings in the spring; hides your solar electric system; and can house your small animals or incubate chickens and ducks.

All disguised to look like a porch on your home, so that desperate and hungry passersby would not have any idea that you have food growing there.

This greenhouse does all that.

You can grow food all year long and no one would know it.

Now that you understand the basics of what the *Secret Greenhouse of Survival* is, and what the benefits of having one are, want to find out HOW YOU can create one for yourself?

Then read on…

CHAPTER-2
STARTING WITH A PLAN

In the Northern Hemisphere, the Sun rises in the east, travels through the southern sky and sets in the west. The sun is higher in the sky (and more intense) during the summer and lowest in the sky during the winter. And the sun is strongest in the middle of the day, when it is due south, during every season.

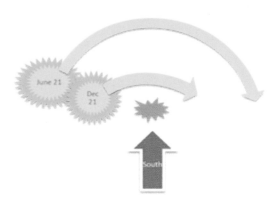

A south facing greenhouse will give you the most solar exposure.

So, just like in a garden, a south facing greenhouse will acquire the greatest amount of sunlight and the greatest amount of solar heat gain. Thus, a south facing greenhouse will provide you with more plant growth, a longer growing season, as well as more heat for your water and more heat for your home in the winter.

Of course we know that most existing homes are not facing perfectly south, but you don't have to have a perfectly south facing wall in order to benefit from creating your own *Secret Greenhouse of Survival*. However, the closer to south your building faces, the better. You may also be able to compensate and have a more south facing greenhouse than your home, by adding a wall extension at an angle to your home, in the right direction.

When reading this book, I will show you the most simple ways to maximize your plant growth and maximize your energy gain for the minimum amount of work and expense. So no matter what your particular situation, this book will give you multiple ideas, tips, and concepts that will help you grow more food and save you money.

One of those concepts is that in any greenhouse you want to maximize your solar exposure by maximizing your "glazing" (glass surfaces). To take full advantage of the sun's energy, you should have glazing in the ceiling above your plant beds (for when the sun is high in the summer sky), as well as glazing on the sides of your building (when the sun is lower in winter).

Concrete walls and rock flooring provide thermal mass to store heat.

Another major concept of the *Secret Greenhouse of Survival* is having sufficient "thermal mass" in the greenhouse to store solar heat. Thermal mass is an object (or objects) that absorb heat during the day and give off heat over a long period of time at night. You can create thermal mass with concrete or rock walls, stored tanks of water, and crushed stone floors.

By having sufficient thermal mas, you will be able to keep plants warmer even during freezing evening temperatures. And keeping your plants warmer gives your plants a longer growing season, and better growth, with no chance of frost or of your plants freezing. Because heat is stored up in your thermal masses, you do not have to pay for energy to maintain an artificial heat source during cold winter months just trying to keep your plants alive.

In addition to a thermal mass, the *Secret Greenhouse of Survival* has insulation in walls and has windows that are highly energy efficient. The windows allow heat and light into the greenhouse, but do not allow it to escape as easily. Insulation in a greenhouse is an almost unheard of concept, as most greenhouses are designed to maximize solar gain during the day, but do very little to maintain heat during cold nights or cloudy days.

Raised planters make it easier for shorter plants to get light from windows and raised planters make it easier for you to work.

The **Secret Greenhouse of Survival** can be highly energy efficient because it uses the latest technology to insulate and uses building materials that will not warp, rot, or mildew in a humid greenhouse environment..

The use of raised (waist height) plant beds is another concept that is key to the **Secret Greenhouse of Survival**. Having raised planters around the edges of your greenhouse makes it easier for you to work in the greenhouse. You don't have to bend over or crawl on your hands and knees in order to inspect and care for your shorter plants. And having raised (waist height) planters allows those plants to get more sun from windows that do not need to reach the floor of the greenhouse in order for shorter plants to get sun.

And because these raised beds are housed in a significant amount of concrete filled block, the beds also add to the thermal mass of the entire greenhouse.

Since the planter beds are about 3 ft. tall, the beds are deep enough for root growth, proper drainage, and soil regeneration- which is not always the case with your typical 6 inch tall outdoor raised beds.

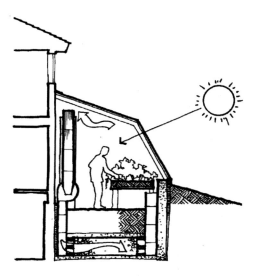

Home connected to greenhouse with raised beds and thermal mass.

This book will also show you how to keep the soil rich in nutrients, without commercial chemical fertilizers, and how you can get 3-4 different seasonal plantings per year in the greenhouse, where you can totally change out your crops, and have 3-4 complete harvests per year.

Another important concept of the **Secret Greenhouse of Survival** is to have a way to control excess heat and humidity in the greenhouse. You can either expel that heat to the outside air to get rid of it; or you may also be able to use this excess heat and humidity your advantage, by using it to heat and to humidify your home in the winter. This can be done quite simply with the use of inexpensive solar powered exhaust fans.

Now that you have the basic concepts and objectives in building a Secret Greenhouse of Survival, we can begin to develop a plan to build your own **Secret Greenhouse of Survival**, tailored to your own individual needs.

The Plan

I have found with any major project, that it is always best to start with a plan. As the old adage goes: "No one plans to fail- they just fail to plan.". Once you do, remember to "make your plan and work your plan".

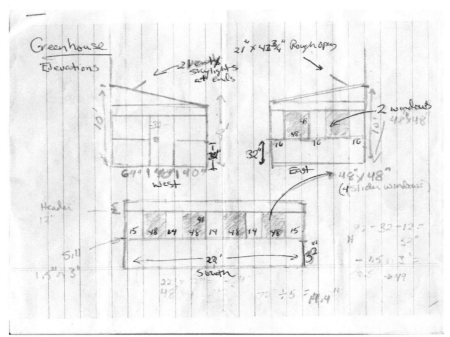

It is always best with any project, to start with a plan.

You will want to figure the location, height, width, length and the materials you will need to create your own Secret Greenhouse of Survival. You will also need to determine the location of the greenhouse in relation to your home and how you will integrate the two buildings.

I have found that it is best to start with a simple drawing and add to the detail from there. You don't have to be an architect. I certainly am not. You just have to understand a little bit about building, and use a little math to figure out your sizes, etc. I will help you as best I can, to show you how you can figure this all out for your own particular situation.

You will want to draw out your elevations and figure out how each side of the building will relate to the other. You will also want to determine your inside dimensions, and how much space your planters will consume, as well as how much room you will comfortably need to work within the greenhouse.

Of course all of these things can be a function of your budget, but luckily the *Secret Greenhouse of Survival* is both relatively inexpensive to build, and provides a high return on your investment in the form of food production, and energy savings.

(For more detailed information on how to figure your own dimensions and building materials requirements, see the **Appendix** at the end of this book. But before you do that, let me take you through the process and show you photos of each step, so that you will have a better idea what you are trying to accomplish, before you get wrapped up in numbers and drawings.)

Costs:

Once you have figured out the dimensions you need to make a list of the materials that you will need as well as the costs of those materials.

If you are not handy, or lack time, you will need to factor in labor costs to do the block work and framing. The job is not complex, but if you are not a "do-it-yourselfer" you may want to hire people with experience to do it for you. I suggest that you can share this book and the diagrams with them, so that they will understand what you are trying to achieve with this project.

Of course, anything you do needs to meet your local building codes, so make sure you have a conversation with a licensed contractor and/or your local building inspector so that you will know what you need to do to meet the building requirements. Remember, this is a greenhouse, so there are often far less restrictions or inspection requirements (if any at all) for a greenhouse building. Just check with your local ordinances.

One other point to consider is that the block work in particular can be less expensive if you have a local professional install it for you. I found that the masons I hired could do the work in less than one day, and the cost for them to do it (including the materials), was cheaper than I could buy just the materials for.

Read through the rest of this book and you will have a better understanding of what you will need for materials, once you see it all together.

Then read the **Appendix**, make a plan of your own, and create a list of materials that will do the job for you.

In the meantime, since any good building starts with a strong foundation, let's begin with that!

CHAPTER-3
BUILDING FROM THE GROUND UP

Once you have developed your plan and decided upon a place to locate your Secret Greenhouse of Survival, you will need to begin the ground work for your construction.

You will should create an open, southerly facing, flat level surface.

Before you begin construction, you will want to create a flat, level, south facing, surface with no trees or other obstructions to block the sunlight into your greenhouse..

You will then need to use wooden stakes, a large tape measure, and string to mark off the corners and sides of where your greenhouse will be located.

Staking Out the Greenhouse Foundation

You will want to measure and stake out the area according to your plan for your foundation.

Start by measuring the east and west walls of your greenhouse from your home to the southern wall (the south facing wall that is furthest from your home). (This is also assuming that your home is going to be the north wall of your greenhouse.) In my case, the east and west side walls were both 12 ft. in length-from the north side home wall to the south side greenhouse wall..

Then drive a wooden stake into the ground at each southern corner. Run a length of string from the corners of your home, to the two wooden stakes that will mark the south corners of your greenhouse.

Next, measure the distance between the two southern corners, to ensure that the south wall will be the proper distance across. (In my case this distance was 22 ft.) If the stakes are too far apart, move them closer together (and vice versa). Then run a length of string to each south facing corner and tie the stakes together.

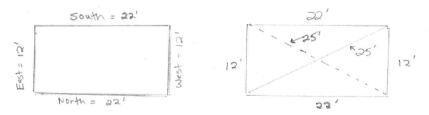

Stake out strings for your walls. Square up by measuring diagonals.

When you stake out the area, you will need to make sure that the corners are square in all directions. It is important that all four corners of your building are "square" (at 90 degree angles) so that all your future block work and wood framing will be square as well.

A simple way to figure this out is by using a little trick where you set up strings or tape measures on the diagonals. When both diagonal measurements are equal, your building is "squared up".

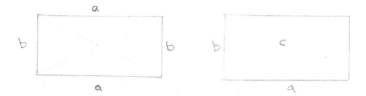

Above "a" is the length, "b" is the width and "c" is the diagonal.

You can also use geometry you can figure out the proper length of the diagonals, in advance of staking them out, by using the formula $a^2 + b^2 = c^2$ where "a" is the length of the building, "b" is the width of the building and "c" is the diagonal (or the hypotenuse of the 90 degree "right" triangle).

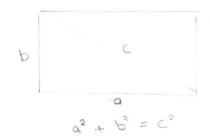

$$a^2 + b^2 = c^2$$

Determine the proper length of the diagonals by using geometry.

Alternatively, you can find websites that will figure it all out for you. For example you can go to: http://www.blocklayer.com/square-layout.aspx (At this website, just submit the lengths of the sides in inches. Once you put in the amounts, you will get the length of the hypotenuse or inside diagonal.)

After you have marked the entire area with string, then you will need to put up some boards along the string on all sides.

Once you have put up boards along the side lines, drive additional wooden stakes in next to the boards. Screw or nail the boards into the wooden stakes in order to secure the boards that are now marking your perimeter. (You should use the wood because it will be sturdier than string when you are digging inside the rectangle to prepare the area for concrete footings.)

Creating Concrete Footings

You can mark where your concrete block is going to run by putting screws in the boards where each course will run for your concrete planters. (Refer to your plan to determine those measurements.)

Put a screw or nail in at the center of each spot and then run a string across to the other side. Now you have a string to mark the centerline of that particular footing. Repeat the process for each planter section and each footing.

Stake boards to mark your perimeter. Then run strings to mark your footings. Then dig out the footing areas to create dirt "forms".

After you have marked where the footings will go, you can dig out the footings at least one foot deep and 16" wide. (You need concrete footings because they add stability to your entire structure and will keep your concrete block walls and planters from sinking or caving in.)

The dug out (deeper) parts in the photo above are the areas where the concrete footings will go. The raised parts create a dirt "form" around the footings to keep the concrete in place while it cures.

You can use board bridges over the dug-out channels to transport the dirt via wheelbarrow out of the area.

Notice that the raised dirt area in the photo is also where the open bottom of each planter will go. (Imagine in the photo that the dug-out areas are now all filled with concrete which will hold the block work on each side of the planters.) By design, there is no concrete poured in these raised dirt areas. This is so that water will drain from inside the planters into the ground. (Proper drainage is important so that plant roots do not get water logged and create "root rot".)

Rebar raised off the ground all the way around the footing gives it strength. Wooden plank bridges can be used to transport dirt.

Once you dig out the channels for the footings run two strands of rebar around the entire area that will be your footer. Where intersections meet, just run rebar over the top of any rebar going in the other direction. Using special metal hangers, raise the rebar off the ground to what will become the center of your footings. This way the concrete can flow underneath the rebar and surround it.

Now you are ready to pour concrete into the footing channels. You obviously can do it yourself, by renting a cement mixer and making your own concrete. Of course, this will take a good deal of time. But it is probably better to pour all the concrete at once, so that it all dries together at the same time. Therefore, I suggest that you hire a professional concrete company and have your concrete premixed and delivered via a cement mixer truck where they can pour the concrete into the channels all at once.

Rebar is sticking up from the poured footing to tie in concrete blocks.

After you have poured the concrete to fill in the footing channels, then level off the concrete with a trowel. Make sure that the footings are level in all directions so that your block walls will be level as well.

While the concrete is setting up and while it is still wet, lay rebar into the footers so that one end of the rebar is sticking up out of the center of the footers. That rebar will later tie in the courses of concrete block to the footer. (Eventually the rebar will stick up through the holes in the courses of block to give the entire structure more stability.)

After the concrete footers are dry and before doing anything further on your greenhouse, take the time to get any window trim, etc. done on your home before you install the greenhouse block work. This will be easier to do now, than it will be after your greenhouse is complete.

Note the pipes in the photo above that are coming through the wall from the home into the greenhouse area. These pipes are for future planter irrigation using grey water, and for solar heated hot water piping going into the home.

Laying Concrete Block

There is not enough room in this book to teach the basics of masonry and running block work, however, you can read up on how to lay concrete block in hundreds of DYI books or on the web. Or, as mentioned previously, you can simply hire someone to do it because in many cases it is cheaper and faster to hire professional masons to lay all your block, than it is for you to just buy the materials.

Lay your concrete block so that each layer is staggered over the other.

When laying the concrete block and using mortar (Portland cement and sand mixture) to hold it all together, stagger your blocks every other course as would be normal in building a concrete block wall. Line up the hole in one end of the top block with the other end of the block underneath it, so you can see down to the footing through all the courses. You will be filling these holes with concrete after the wall is built in order to make it a solid concrete wall and to give it even more strength and stability.

When laying the block, leave enough space to frame in an exterior door at the west end, and leave space in the block planter for a door going into the home.

Notice the plumbing pipes are "roughed in" so that they are coming through the wall into the greenhouse from the home in the photo above. The two smaller pipes are a ¾" cold water PVC pipe coming out of the home and a ¾" hot water PVC pipe from the greenhouse going back into the home. The larger 2" PVC pipe is for grey water coming out of the home into the green house, just above the beginning of the U shaped planter.

2 ft. wide planters of concrete block surround the greenhouse walls.

Tape plastic around the pipes to keep bugs and construction debris out of the pipes while you are finishing off the greenhouse. (Note how the 2" PVC grey water pipe in upper middle of picture above comes out from the home just over the end of the U shaped planter.)

Once all the block is laid, you will have 2 ft. wide planters in a U shape all the way around the greenhouse perimeter.

Also note the GFI exterior electrical outlet on the wall under the 2" pipe. You will want electricity on occasion in the greenhouse (although you won't need much of it) for incubation lamps, etc. The electric power will need to be on a GFI (Ground Fault Interrupt) circuit to avoid electrical shocks in a wet environment.

Concrete poured in the block with lug bolts to hold the wood frame.

Fill the holes in the block with poured concrete (to make a solid concrete wall). Place lug bolts (inserted while the concrete is wet) to attach the 2" x 6" bottom plate and window sill that will be connected to the wooden framing (see Chapter 4- Wood Framing).

When the concrete is dry, you can use a liquid concrete sealant to protect the concrete from decay over time. Apply this sealant with a paint roller. (Note: Do not use a tar based sealant inside the concrete planters. You don't want poison in your dirt, plants and food.)

Fill the planters with layers of stone, branches, clay, dirt and mulch.

Once the block wall is finished and cured, fill the planter 6 inches deep with crushed stone. Then put a 6 inch layer of tree limbs on top of the stone. After that, put in 6 inches of clay, then 6 inches of dirt and then 6 inches of mulch. All of these layers will work together to decompose and add nutrients to your planter. (Do not fill your planter all the way to the top until the grey water piping has been run. See Chapter 7- Plumbing.)

After the planters have been filled, then fill in 4-6 inches of crushed stone on what will be the floor of your greenhouse. This stone is for drainage and to also add to the thermal mass (heat collection) of the greenhouse. Bring in the stone before you start framing the walls, as it will be much easier to do this now, than it would be when the walls are all up.

Now that the concrete is complete, it is time to start on your building's wood framing.

CHAPTER-4
I'VE BEEN FRAMED!

Once the block wall is complete and you have your crushed rock on the floor and your growing medium (rock, branches, dirt, mulch) in the planters, it is time to start the wood framing. Unlike a stand-alone building, you are only going to need to construct 3 walls-because the 4th wall is actually the wall of your existing home!

The home provides a sturdy 4th wall on which to attach your frame.

This gives you a big cost and labor savings.. and you can start with a sturdy foundation to bolt your greenhouse framing onto.

Build the frame for each wall on the ground according to your plan and as you would do with traditional framing. (Again, there is not enough room in this book to teach basic carpentry or how to build a wooden wall frame. But of course, you can look it up in any DYI book or website, or you can hire someone to do it.)

To keep your building lumber from decaying over time, you should only use pressure treated lumber in the construction of this project, since your wood will be in a continually wet environment in the greenhouse.

Even though your pressure treated lumber will be supposedly kiln dried, a lot of this lumber is still wet to the touch when you buy it from your hardware store. Try to get pressure treated lumber that is as dry as possible to start with. This is because once the wood is in place as part of the greenhouse, it will go through a tremendous amount of heating, cooling, expansion and contraction. If your wood is too wet when you build your framing, it will dry out in the hot environment of the greenhouse and it will shrink and become shorter than when you put the wood in place. That can cause a lot of wood splitting and shrinkage that could be a problem for you later.

We used 2" x 6" wall studs for the construction of our walls. This gave us extra strength over 2' x 4" construction and also allowed us more insulation. We used 2" x 10" pressure treated lumber for the ceiling joists. This was adequate to hold our skylights and our glazed roof and was load bearing for snow, etc. Of course, you should find out the building code requirements in your area before you start construction.

Another tip is to make sure to use galvanized nails and deck screws that will not corrode in the wet environment and when used with pressure treated wood. The last thing you want is to have your nails or screws break off due to corrosion.

When you start your wall frames, I suggest that you start with the east side wall. Build the wall on the ground by first framing in the 2" x 10" window headers. Frame in the rough openings for the windows and attach the bottom plate and top plate of the frame. Drill holes in the bottom plate where the concrete bolts will go through. Use Liquid Nails to glue the bottom plate to the concrete as you would for any bottom plate attached to a concrete slab or wall. Lift the wall into place and then bolt the wall to the concrete with washers and nuts. Screw the north side of the east frame into the frame of the house wall for additional support.

Next, put up the framed wall with the windows on the south side.

Then using the same steps, build the frame for the south side wall. Drill holes where the bolts in the concrete will come through the bottom plate. Spread Liquid Nails on the bottom (concrete) side of the bottom plate. Lift the wall into place. Level and square everything off and then screw in temporary cross bracing to hold both walls together and everything in place. Then screw and nail the east and the south wall frames together. Bolt down the bottom plate to the concrete block.

Once these two walls are up, you can begin working on the ceiling joists that will go from north to south (from your home to your southern greenhouse wall) to hold up your roof.

Since you will already have mulch and dirt in the planters, I suggest that you place cardboard and plastic sheeting inside the planters so that you will not get pressure treated saw dust (which does not break down) as well as nails and other construction debris in your growing beds.

Once you begin working on the ceiling, you can set up your ladders on your planters, so that you can reach the areas you will need to work on when constructing the ceiling joists.

Put cardboard and plastic inside the planter beds to protect your soil and mulch from construction debris, screws, sawdust , etc.

As with any framing project, having a compressed air nail gun is not a bad idea. You can drive the nails in with one pull of the trigger, which is important when you are trying to hold boards, ceiling joists and walls in place.

I also highly recommend my favorite screws for any construction project. Those screws are called Star Drive screws. For framing I usually use 2 ½" screws as they will hold two 2 x 4s or 2 x 6s together without coming through the other side. Also the fact that they are exterior screws means that they will not corrode in any framing environment.

The star head pattern helps you drive the screws in without stripping them which is all too often the case with flat head or Philips-head screws. And they are easy to back out too, so if you make a mistake (which I have been known to do) you can take out the screws and fix it, without having to scrap your valuable wood.

You can also get a magnetic screw drive guide that holds the screw straight and that slides away from the screw the further you drive it in. This allows you to screw in the screws from numerous positions and keeps your screws from going off at an angle, or popping out from your screw driver/drill before you can get them into the wood.

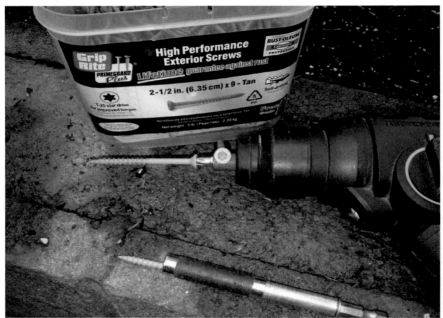

Star Drive screws have a star head that works better than flat head or Philips-head screws. And a magnetic screw drive guide can keep your screws going in straight using only one hand to hold the drill.

Since I discovered these screws every project has gone faster, and been stronger as a result. (I have often said that I could build anything with enough lumber and enough star drive screws.)

To begin constructing your ceiling joists, take a 2 x 10 board and screw it into the home wall (the back/ north wall of the greenhouse) at the height of your greenhouse roof (according to your plan.) Make sure that it is level. Use lag bolts to further secure the board(s) to the wall.

Place joist hangers at the distance of your joists apart from each other according to your plan. (My ceiling joists were 16" on center.) Place the ceiling joists in the hangers and then lay the other end of each joist on top of the south wall. Make sure that the south end of each joist is also 16" on center and then nail these in place using hurricane clips.

Lag bolt a 2 x 10 board to the frame of the house. Use ceiling joist hangers to hold 2 x 10 ceiling joists which will run from the exterior home wall to the south wall of greenhouse.

Once ceiling joist are strung across, attach a board along the front (south side) to tie in all the joists, and to make a soffit.

Once your clips are in place on the north side and the south side of the greenhouse, you can start placing all your ceiling joists and nailing or screwing them in place. Make sure to use galvanized nails and/or exterior deck screws that will not corrode in the wet environment or when used with pressure treated lumber.

Once all your ceiling joists are in place you can tie them all together with a board running across the front (south side) of the greenhouse. This board will also become your front soffit once you cover it with fascia and siding.

Then frame in a box (according to the manufacturer's rough-in dimensions) to hold your vented skylights in place. (You can get the rough-in frame dimensions from the literature that comes with your skylights.)

Frame in your boxes to hold the vented skylights. The skylights will be inserted after your roof covering is put into place.

Once this is done you can frame in the final (west) wall. Make sure to allow for the rough-in dimensions of your exterior door frame.

Also make sure that all your work is square and the walls are level. Make the necessary corrections (if you have any) now before moving to the next step.

Finished Frame With Decomposed Mulch in the Foreground.

Now that your frame is finished, you are ready to put on your roofing material.

CHAPTER-5
ROOF, ROOF!

The roof of your *Secret Greenhouse of Survival* has to work like any other roof on any other greenhouse. You will need to be able to keep out the elements, while you also get the maximum amount of light into greenhouse so that you can maximize your plant growth.

These polycarbonate panels were designed for use on a greenhouse.

Even though it will be letting in light, you will need to have a roof material that is strong, and that keeps heat in and cold out.

Of course your greenhouse roofing material will also need to be water proof, and have the ability to be load bearing so that snow will not break it.

The material will need to be wind resistant, and not break or lift off your ceiling joists in gale force winds. And it will also have to be flexible enough so to be able to withstand continual expansion and contraction from heat and cold.

The Thermaglas mulit-wall polycarbonate panel pictured above is designed for greenhouses and it can withstand all the problems mentioned above.

Also, from a prepper standpoint- a greenhouse roof needs to be discrete. You do not want the roof to be a dead give-away to passersby that the attached room is actually a greenhouse with food growing there.

Polycarbonate panels have channels running through them that give it strength and insulating qualities.

This polycarbonate panel is totally unobtrusive and is not obvious from the side of the building once it is installed. Thus, the panel helps to keep your greenhouse camouflaged and allows you to hide your food production in plain sight, so that no one from the street will be able to tell that you have food growing there.

Polycarbonate panels are custom cut to run the entire length of the roof.

There are channels running down the length of these polycarbonate panels that add strength, and allow for insulation, ventilation, and expansion. As a result, the panels can withstand a tremendous amount of weight from snow loads and can also withstand extremes of temperature, as well as expansion and contraction when used in a greenhouse environment..

The panels are custom cut and shipped from the factory to run the entire length of the roof and are 4 ft. wide. My panels where 13 ft. long to allow for sufficient overhang beyond the soffit.

I ordered my panels at the International Greenhouse Company located in Eden Prairie, MN. They did a good job and these people have always treated me right.

Special screws, washers and neoprene gaskets are available to hold the polycarbonate panels in place.

Although my 4' x 13' panels where not particularly heavy, they were difficult to maneuver, being so long and so wide.. And since they are so light weight and have such a large surface area, I found from experience that the panels make excellent "sails" in the wind. So I suggest that you do not try to install these panels on a windy day. It will only frustrate you and you may also end up breaking, or damaging your panels.

When installing the panels, note that there is a top and a bottom side. The top side has a protective film on it that you remove later. The top also has a UV coating so that the plastic will not deteriorate in the sun.

The panel ribs run top to bottom and the panels are cut to the full length of the roof so there will be no joints between the top and the bottom and thus, no leaks. Follow the instructions for installation and screw the panels into your ceiling joists as per the instructions provided with the panels. Channel joints between the individual panels hold the panels together and allow for expansion (in hot weather) and contraction (in cold weather) and seal the joint to keep rain water out.

Use galvanized screws that are made for the job, as standard screws cannot hold up under the extreme stress of heat, humidity and cold.

Get the special screws and washers with neoprene (rubber) gaskets that will protect the polycarbonate from cracking and that will seal the screw hole in the polycarbonate from bugs and water seepage. You can predrill holes in the polycarbonate to keep the plastic from cracking before you screw the screws into the wood frame. (Note the predrilled hole in the photo above and also note the rubber gasket on the screw.)

Make sure that you use galvanized screws. Over a period of time a great deal of stress is put on these screws, as the panels go through expansion from heat and contraction from cold. The greenhouse is also a "hostile" environment for non-treated metal screws, since there is such high humidity in a greenhouse.

Once you have all your polycarbonate panels in place, next you will need to install your vented, deck-mounted skylights onto the roof over the skylight framing that you created during the roof framing process.

Keep in mind that unlike a traditional shingled roof, your deck mounted skylight will not have shingles surrounding them, so you will need to purchase a metal flashing kit to go around each skylight. (You also may want to have precut the holes for the skylights in the polycarbonate roof panels, prior to installation, so that you can avoid breaking the panels when cutting them on the roof for the skylight.)

Vented skylight on top of polycarbonate roofing material; and solar panel for greenhouse solar fan is hidden from view of passersby.

Aside from the metal flashing kits, the skylights come with a flexible flashing that has a sticky substance on the bottom that will adhere to the roof and seal out water and ice from entering under the skylight. I also used a considerable amount of clear silicone caulking around the skylights and the flashing kits to ensure a good seal. You may want to go back over these seals after your first summer season, since expansion may pull away the silicone over time. You can apply additional silicone in any areas that appear to be leaking and seal them off before winter. This is important since you will want to make sure that water does not get up underneath the skylight and the polycarbonate panels since water expands when it freezes and could loosen the seals and make for more leaks into your greenhouse.

View from under the skylight in the greenhouse. You can open the skylight for ventilation of high heat at the top of the greenhouse.

Once installed, the skylights can be opened from inside to allow ventilation and the escape of excessive heat in the greenhouse. As illustrated future chapters, this greenhouse is extremely efficient and heat cannot escape unless you allow it to. This can create a huge build-up of heat, which if unchecked can cause your plants to wilt. I learned this from experience when I came back one day from town after having the newly constructed greenhouse closed up on a sunny day in February. Even though the outside temperature was below freezing, the internal greenhouse temperature upon my return was over 120 degrees F.

Based on the weather outlook each day, you can plan accordingly to allow for more or less ventilation by simply opening and closing the skylights to various degrees. During the summer, my skylights pretty much are open all the time, day and night.

Also, make sure that you get skylights with insect screens to keep unwanted insects out of the greenhouse. And treat yourself to the long handled opening rod that allows you to adjust and open the windows from the greenhouse floor, without having to find a ladder every time you want to open or adjust the windows.

An insect screen keeps unwanted bugs out of the greenhouse and a special rod allows you to open the windows without a ladder.

Now that you have completed the roof and skylights, you are ready for siding, doors and windows.

CHAPTER-6
WINDOWS, AND DOORS, AND SIDING- OH MY!

Now that you have the frame and the roof finished, you can install the windows, doors and siding for the greenhouse. I used argon gas filled energy efficient windows that would allow thermal gain during the day time and keep heat from escaping at night.

Greenhouse with doors, windows, and cement board siding and trim.

My windows also slide open to allow me to be able to get maximum light, sun and breeze through the greenhouse when I needed to do so.

You can use exterior siding and trim that matches your home, but I would highly recommend that you use a cement board (as I did) for the exterior siding and interior paneling. This is because the cement board siding is impervious to bugs, and will not warp or deteriorate under the extreme heat, cold and humid conditions associated with a greenhouse.

The completed greenhouse from street level just looks like an add-on room.

I used metal insulated exterior doors for both the exterior door going out of the greenhouse into the garden, and for the door going into the home from the greenhouse.

I used these metal doors because they can tolerate the extremes of high heat and high humidity in a greenhouse without warping or rotting. The metal doors also are more secure than a wooden door, and as a preparedness minded individual, I am always looking for ways that my family, home and my food supply can be more secure.

6 panel metal insulated exterior door.

In addition to the metal exterior door that swings in to the greenhouse from out of doors, I installed a metal screen security door that provides additional security and allows me to leave the screen door open at night without fear of an intruder breaking in.

These security doors are installed on the outside and swing out. They are installed using a one-way screw bolt system that allows you to only screw in the hinges and does not allow an intruder to unscrew the frame and door in order to get into the building.

The security door also has a steal deadbolt lock that requires a key to open it from either side, so that people cannot smash or cut through the door screen in order to simply turn a deadbolt and let themselves in.

The thick metal screen of the security door is welded to the door frame and is unique in that it is small enough to keep out bugs, but also thick enough to keep out raccoons, opossums, foxes and people. This security during the day and evening is important because at any one time I may be growing food, or housing livestock in the greenhouse.

This door works. I have had raccoons try to get into the greenhouse to eat baby ducks that I was incubating in the greenhouse. But bite, scratch and claw as they might, the raccoons could not get through.

Although it looks decorative, the security door has welded steel bars and a thick welded metal screen that will not allow intruders inside.

Once the windows, doors, exterior walls and trim are installed, you can paint the walls and trim with the same colors as the home, so that it will all blend in.

Prior to installing interior walls, you should consider filling in the gaps

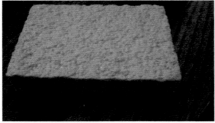 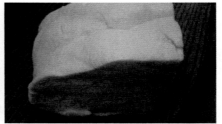

Closed Cell foam insulation.   **Open Cell foam insulation.**

with insulation to keep the greenhouse as energy efficient as possible. You can use a professionally sprayed in foam, of which there are basically two major types. One is called "closed cell foam" and the other is called "open cell foam". The closed cell foam is rigid and works well with wet environments, but does not expand and contract, thus leaving potential gaps for air to come in.

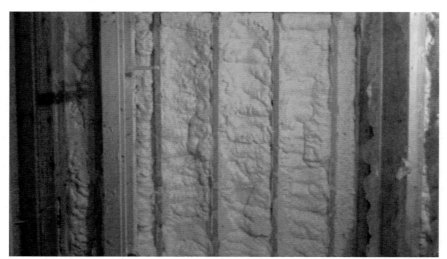

You can use spray in foam insulation to insulate the walls of your greenhouse.

Open cell foam is spongy and sticks to the surfaces it was sprayed to, and expands and contracts with heat and cold, thus keeping air from moving in and out of the greenhouse.

You can also use a rigid foam that you can buy at the hardware store, and then use spray in foam (from the can) to fill in the gaps and to seal any spaces and cracks between the insulation and your framing.

You can use rigid foam foil backed insulation that comes in sheets.

For budgetary reasons, and since my area between the windows was so small, I used a foil backed rigid foam insulation as well as other insulation that will not rot in high humidity to fill in the frames between the windows.

Even though we have had sub-zero temperatures during winter months, my greenhouse has never gotten below 45 degrees in the evening time.

And I also used spray in foam from the can, to fill in the gaps. All this will makes your greenhouse more efficient and keeps you from having to use supplemental heat to keep your plants from freezing on extremely cold nights.

Painted cement wall board and window trim inside the greenhouse.

Once you have the insulation installed, you will want to use the same cement board exterior siding inside the greenhouse. Due to high humidity and water usage (through spray hoses, etc.), using cement board exterior siding will ensure that the greenhouse walls will remain impervious to the elements, both internal and external.

I also recommend that you use PVC trim board for the window sill trim inside the greenhouse, as PVC will hold up better and be more resistant to water than anything else you could use. And since I use my window sills inside the greenhouse to grow plants in pots, that is important.

Now just use silicone caulking between all the joints, and then paint your siding and trim, and you will have an enclosed and insulated building that is ready for greenhouse plumbing.

CHAPTER-7
A PLUMBING WEE WILL GO

Of course since you are building a greenhouse to grow plants, those plants will need water. One way to water your plants and to also be more sustainable, is to use your household grey water to provide water for your plants. Grey water is the drain water from your lavatory sinks, washing machine, and bath tubs. (Basically anything except water from toilets-also known as "black water"- can be used.)

You can use drain water from your home to feed greenhouse plants.

You can also use the drain water from your kitchen sink, as long as you strain out food particles and do not use a garbage disposal. However, any water that you use, cannot contain bleach or other such chemicals, since those would harm your plants. (Normal soap that you use for cleaning yourself and your dishes for the most part is OK to use on plants.) So understand also that this means you cannot clean your sinks, tubs, etc. with bleach, or you will kill the plants in your greenhouse, as well as many of the micro-organisms in the soil that help those plants to grow. The same goes for drain cleaners. Don't use them with water that goes into your greenhouse. (Honestly, where would you be getting commercial chemicals to clean sinks and drains in a grid-down situation anyway?)

That being said, using grey water allows you grow plants by recycling water that would otherwise end up in a septic system or municipal sewer. This recycling lowers your total consumption of water, and your need to use electricity to pump that water from the ground, and into your house. In a grid down situation, you will need to minimize your total water consumption, since you will need that water for drinking, cooking, etc. The more water that you can recycle, the less you need to use.

PVC pipe can run from your drains to the wall of your greenhouse.

By connecting 2" PVC pipe to an existing grey water drain (from a lavatory sink, for example) you can run this 2" pipe down to your greenhouse and have it go through the wall into the greenhouse so that the grey water can feed your plant beds. You may want to have 2:" ball valves in the PVC line that allow you to change the flow of the water going into the greenhouse, so that the grey water can be switched back to your septic system and vice versa. This allows you the option to choose the direction you want the water to flow, so that if your plants are getting too much water, you can divert the water back to the septic system.

When figuring how to run your pipe to the greenhouse, insure that any straight runs flow downhill to the tune of ¼" to the foot, so that water and any particulate waste will run in the right direction. (You don't want your grey water flowing in the wrong direction and you also don't want to be dealing with clogs- especially in a grid down situation. You will have enough to deal with as it is.)

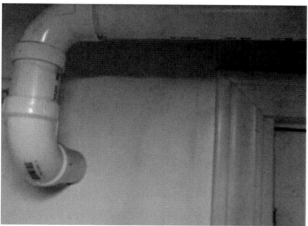

Grey water flows out to the greenhouse from inside the home.

Once you come to the "end of the line" you will need to cut a hole going from the inside wall, out to the greenhouse, making sure you do not cut through any existing plumbing, wiring, and house frame. I cut this hole and put a pipe through the wall, prior to completion of the greenhouse, and prior to hooking up the grey water to it, but of course that takes some careful calculations in advance. Also, you want to be sure that any pipes you have coming through the wall prior to connection are temporarily plugged in order to keep insects, heat and cold from entering into your home through the unconnected pipes.

Measure both the interior and exterior walls carefully so that when you cut the hole, your drain pipe comes out over your planter. You will then want to connect your house grey water piping to a perforated 2" drainpipe in your greenhouse that will run along the top or be buried slightly under the dirt in the planters. (You can create your own perforated 2" PVC pipe by simply drilling holes every 8" or so in the sides of a regular 2" PVC pipe.)

Once again you will want to make sure that the pipe runs all the way around the beds of your planter, at a ¼" per foot downward slope, so that water will flow all the way to the end.

You may want to wrap that perforated pipe in a drain cloth that is used for outdoor drains, to allow water to drain, but prevents rodents, roots and dirt from clogging your pipe.

Grey water pipe from the home going into the plant beds. Note the clean out and the black drain cloth wrapped around the perforated pipe in the planter.

You will also want to make sure you have a "T-Y" connection and clean out just before the house pipe goes into the drain pipe for the planter beds, so that you will be able to run a plumber's snake through the pipe, in case you do have a clog in the bed pipe. (Again, you don't want that grey water backing up into your house sinks.) You should probably consider another clean out at the very end of the pipe run as well, so that you can have a place to push the snake through and so you can have a place for the clog to go.

Dain plug at the very end of the bed pipe to clean out potential clogs.

Creating Hot Water in Your Greenhouse

Since your greenhouse will provide abundant passive solar heat on sunny days, you can use your greenhouse to preheat hot water for your home. You can also eliminate highly inefficient hot water tanks that heat up large quantities of water, and then cool down (giving off heat to their surroundings 24 hours a day) only to need to be reheated when the water temperature inside the tank drops below a certain hot threshold temperature. That constant heating and reheating of water, which for the most part is only used at certain times in the day, is a huge waste of energy. That is energy that you will not have, should we have a grid-down scenario. Standard hot water heaters are also a waste of energy in that they release heat to their surroundings year round, which can require you to use additional energy to cool your home during summer heat. Thus, traditional water heaters waste energy in two ways- 1) you are spending money for heat that escapes from the water tank, and 2) you have to use even more energy to cool off the air that has been heated up by the escaping tank heat.

In my system, you can preheat your house water through a series of black water pipe coils that have direct access to the sun's rays at the top of the greenhouse. That preheated water may be plenty hot for your purposes (cooking, showering, cleaning dishes) as it comes out of the greenhouse on a hot sunny day. If it is not quite hot enough (due to a cloudy day, etc.) you can instantly boost the water temperature as the water goes by in the pipe by using what is called a "tankless hot water heater". A tankless heater is basically a water heater that is inline of your hot water piping and heats the water as it goes by. Thus a tankless heater eliminates the need for a standing body of 40-80 gallons of preheated hot water (which, as we said, gives off heat even when not in use, to its surroundings).

Tankless hot water heaters today are small and super-efficient.

Tankless hot water heaters today are extremely efficient and only use electricity as the hot water is needed. These "on demand" water heaters can be placed at the beginning of the hot water line in your house so that one tankless heater can heat all your hot water, or, if you have long pipe runs and many people using water at the same time, you can place individual tankless heaters under each sink or bathtub. This allows you to only heat the hot water, for that use, *as you need it.*

Tankless hot water heaters require 220V wiring and circuit (just like a regular hot water heater). So just like a regular hot water heater, you should consider the tankless hot water heater as a convenience, and as something that will probably not function when there is no electricity for whatever reason. That is why I consider my tankless hot water heater to be a backup or "boost" to my solar hot water. Note that the solar heating of my hot water does most of the work of taking the water which comes out of my well at about 40-45 degrees F, up to 100+ degrees in my greenhouse. Most people can take a shower comfortably in water that is that temperature and most cleaning of pots and pans can done at 140 degrees or less. More heat than that can burn or scald a person, so most standard water heaters are set below that temperature.

You can also set the temperature on a tankless hot water heater, so that you only heat water that is below a certain temperature coming out of your greenhouse. Thus, if the water is hot enough using the sun alone, then the tankless hot water heater uses no energy. If the water is not quite warm enough coming out of the greenhouse, the tankless heater boosts the temperature up to the desired temperature you have set.

A tankless hot water heater attached to a ceiling joist, will boost the hot water for your house.

It is important to note that standard PVC water pipe today may not be able to handle the on demand high water temperatures instantly coming out of your hot water heater. The immediate heat can make thin piping expand and contract to the point where some PVC fittings will loosen or crack over time when screwed onto hot brass fittings. That is why in the photo above, I have flexible ¾" pipe between the hot water coming out of the tankless heater and into the PVC hot water line. This allows for dissipation of a little heat, as well as expansion and contraction of the metal fittings that will not fail, like PVC fittings will in close proximity to the tankless heater.

Also notice in the photo above, that the preheated water from my greenhouse comes in from the left of the picture frame and goes into the tankless hot water heater as "cold water". Note also that the hot water comes out of the tankless heater through the flexible metal pipes and goes back into the hot water line "upstream" from the greenhouse. Also notice that I have a series of valves that prevent the hot water from going back "downstream" toward the greenhouse and that those valves also allow me to bypass the tankless heater altogether, which I have done often throughout the summer months, and which you will want to be able to do when you have no electricity to use the tankless heater.

Cold water coming into the greenhouse (left) and hot water leaving the greenhouse (from black pipe on right).

Just like you have done for the 2" grey water pipe, you will need to bring a cold water pipe through the wall into the greenhouse from your home. Likewise you will need to have piping to take the preheated hot water from the greenhouse back through the wall, and into your home's hot water supply (that can then be boosted by your tankless hot water heater).

The same as when using a standard hot water heater, you need to have an expansion tank in the cold water line (blue tank in the above photo), prior to heating the water in the greenhouse. This tank will allow the water to expand as it gets hot, so you won't have bursting hot water pipes in your greenhouse. The standard pressure relief valve on these expansion tanks will also keep the tank from exploding, should the water get too hot.

I also put in a series of valves that give me the option of diverting water for other purposes in the future (including taking showers, and doing laundry in the greenhouse) should we have a total grid down situation and I have to use gravity (instead of an electric pump) to move water through the pipes.

Pressurized cold water in the greenhouse can be used for multiple purposes.

The valves also give me the opportunity to have pressurized cold water in the greenhouse to wash tools, spray down buckets, fill animal watering dishes and to generally use in the course of working in the greenhouse. Notice the retractable hose on the wall. The hose stretches from one end of the greenhouse to the other, which makes it invaluable for spraying down leaves of citrus trees or watering potted plants in the greenhouse.

Coils of black water pipe absorb heat in the greenhouse for hot water.

There are a number of ways that you could preheat hot water for your home in a greenhouse, but to me, simpler is better. So I attached a metal shelf to the back wall of the greenhouse and created a wooden frame which I attached to the ceiling joists of the greenhouse to hold standard 1" plastic water pipe in 100' coils. I attached each of these in series with a coupling so that water would flow through and get heated as it passed through the hot black coils that sit near the ceiling in the greenhouse. Being close to the top of the greenhouse provides direct solar heat from the sun's rays and also heat from the hot air at the top of the greenhouse. The water in the coils heats up during the day, and by mid-day to evening time, that water can be hot enough to take showers and wash dishes.

I used 8 coils (800 ft.) of pipe that provide more than 20 gallons of hot water when needed. Even on cold sunny days, there is plenty of hot water for our purposes, and if you schedule showers and washing chores accordingly, you can use 40-60 gallons of solar heated hot water for free each day before the sun goes down. All that hot water is without using electricity, except for pumping the water through the pipes of the house, and even that can be done with a 12 volt pump that can run off of solar power or a 12 volt battery that can be recharged by solar power.

Once the water is heated in the greenhouse, that hot water flows into the house as soon as you turn on a faucet, and you can boost the heat of that water by running it through a regular hot water heater, or through a tankless hot water heater as discussed previously in this chapter. Or you can bypass any artificial heat source altogether, and let the sun do all the work for free.

A solar shower and a pump sprayer can also provide hot water under pressure in your greenhouse.

An even simpler hot water solution is to have a solar water collection bag, that heats a limited amount of hot water hanging in your greenhouse.

These bags are often used for camping showers, and although they do not supply much water, they are a psychological pleasure compared to using cold water. They are gravity fed, so they do not produce much pressure, however you can pour the heated water into a clean garden pump spray can, and then use that for hot water under pressure to take showers and clean dishes.

Rainwater Collection

You can go through an great deal of water when growing plants or starting seedlings in your greenhouse. But you will need that water, if you expect your plants to grow.

In a grid down situation, water will be an even more valuable resource and you may not have enough energy to pump everything you need out of a well. But rainwater harvesting can be an easy and reliable way to have water on hand for your plants.

You simply need to collect the water that naturally falls on your greenhouse roof, by having a gutter at the low side of the greenhouse roof, and have that gutter run into a rain barrel.

The tank pictured below uses food grade plastic that does not leach chemicals into the water and that could be used for potable (drinking) water for you and your family if necessary. (Of course you don't want to be using petrochemical agents in any water that you use to grow your plants either, since eventually you would be eating those poisons when you consume the plants.) The tank is also colored, so that light cannot get in and so that algae cannot grow in the water.

This tank holds 485 gallons of water and when empty, the tank can fill with water with less than an inch of rain falling on my greenhouse roof. You can find smaller and larger tanks, but keep in mind that the top of the tank has to be below the lowest point on your greenhouse roof so that rain water will flow downhill from the gutters into your collection tank.

That much water (485 gallons) collected after every rainfall can go a long way toward making your greenhouse self-sustaining, and can provide your plants with water even after the worst natural or man-made disasters. Furthermore, having well watered plants that are growing inside of a secure building, will provide your family with food and security even in the worst of times.

Rain water collection tank connected to the gutter from your greenhouse roof.

Make sure the tank is level and does not sit on any sharp objects that could puncture the bottom of the tank. (All my rain water collection tanks sit on thin concrete pavers or on 4" thick cement slabs that I had poured for that purpose.)

In fact, you may want to consider pouring a cement slab for your greenhouse rainwater collection tank at the same time that you pour concrete for your footers, etc. (during the early stage of the greenhouse construction process). That will be easier and more cost effective than doing it later.

CHAPTER-8
PREPARING THE NURSERY FOR BABY PLANTS

Now that your **Secret Greenhouse of Survival** is secure, and you have several sources of water, you can prepare your greenhouse for planting. Since you have run your grey water piping all around your planters, you can now fill in the last 6-12" of space in those planters with garden soil and decomposed mulch.

After you have run your grey water pipes, fill in your planter with garden soil and good decomposed mulch.

Use the remainder of your decomposed mulch to top off the beds.

Just as in the *Secret Garden of Survival*, I advocate using good decomposed mulch that will provide your greenhouse plant beds with nutrients and active microorganisms that will feed your plants and protect your soil from drying out.

Good decomposed mulch will arrive with an acrid smell, and should be hot and steaming as it comes off the truck. This means that the microorganisms are working to breakdown the bio mass, and that the soil and mulch should be full of nutrients.

Also, as I mentioned in my book *Secret Garden of Survival- How to Grow a Camouflaged Food-Forest*, be careful about where you get your decomposed mulch. You need to know where your mulch comes from. You do not want to get "free mulch" from a municipality for example, because it very well could have come from roadside debris, that in many cases was sprayed with herbicide before it was cut and mulched. That herbicide can stay in the mulch and seep into your soil and potentially could prevent plants from growing in your plant beds for the next five years!

Seed your planters with a good nitrogen fixer like clover.

After your garden soil and mulch is spread, you should establish a ground cover crop that will also help get the microorganisms working to help your other plants grow. Therefore I recommend that you seed your beds with clover which will take root immediately and which has the benefit of also being a "nitrogen fixer". A nitrogen fixer is a plant that takes nitrogen from the air and makes it available for the other plants around it. Thus nitrogen fixers are nature's natural fertilizer, and it is recommended that 60 percent of crops in a truly sustainable garden, be cover crops that fix nitrogen, such as clover, mustard and buckwheat, or legumes that are also nitrogen fixers, such as peanuts, beans, and peas.

Once your nitrogen fixing plants are established, you can interplant your other vegetables, and leafy greens, etc. without pulling up or removing the cover crop. Just leave the clover in place and the plants will all work in a symbiotic relationship, where each does better together, than they do by themselves.

You will want to make sure that anything that you plant in your beds is watered on a regular basis until it is established enough to put down roots that can reach your grey water (that leaches into the soil).

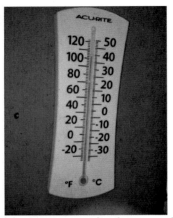

Temperatures in the greenhouse can reach over 100 degrees F.

Since you have built an extremely energy efficient greenhouse, you may experience that it might become too hot for your plants unless the windows, screen door, and vents are open in the heat of the day. As I mentioned earlier, your greenhouse can reach temperatures of well over 100 degrees F if left closed up. That kind of intense heat can wilt plants, and have an adverse effect on you and any animals that might shelter in your greenhouse in the future.

One automatic and sustainable solution to that problem is installing a solar powered exhaust fan in your greenhouse. Such a fan, only runs when the sun is out, and runs faster, the more intense the sun's rays are.

You can purchase solar exhaust fans (often marketed as solar attic exhaust fans) at your major big box home improvement retailer.

My fan came with a 10 watt solar panel that sits on my greenhouse roof and plugs into the installed fan. It runs quietly and can move a lot of air.

Installing these fans is relatively easy since they are designed to fit into an air channel inside the normal 16" on center stud spacing. (In other words, they fit between the studs which are actually 14½" apart.) Once you determine where your studs are (using a stud finder, for example) you can mark the height that you want the fan (higher is better, since heart rises). You can then cut out a hole in the inside panel and then box off a square that is 14½" x 14½". This is the box that your hot air will be sucked through from inside of your greenhouse to the cooler air outside.

Creating a box through the wall for a solar powered exhaust fan will cool the greenhouse using the power of the sun.

The entire fan assembly is attached to the outside wall directly over the air channel. Once the assembly is screwed to the exterior wall, all you have to do is plug in the solar panel, and you instantly have a solar powered fan that will move air through your greenhouse automatically (and at no power cost to you) on hot sunny days.

I recommend using silicone sealant where the fan mounts to the exterior wall in order to keep out weather and bugs. Also, I recommend stapling a metal insect window screen on the inside of the boxed in area, to prevent bugs from flying or crawling into the greenhouse, and to keep bugs from being sucked through the fan from inside the greenhouse.

The entire solar fan assembly attaches to the outside wall.

During the hot summer days, I run the exterior solar fan to prevent the building from becoming too hot. During the winter I use a second solar fan which I installed to suck hot humid air out of the greenhouse and into my home.

We use another solar fan to bring heat and humidity into the home from the greenhouse during the cold winter months.

When not in use, I put insulation behind the fan in the greenhouse to keep the home air constant. (Note- we removed the fan cover in the photos above for purposes of demonstration.)

Thus, during cold, dry winter days, I can take excess heat and humidity from the greenhouse (using solar power) to provide more comfortable warm and humid air inside my home. At night I close a cover to the fan inside the greenhouse, and we remain "toasty" in the home, no matter what the external temperature.

Another added benefit of bringing in greenhouse air into the home is that it has a high oxygen content, since plants naturally give off oxygen and consume carbon dioxide (the opposite of people and animals). So breathing in what plants exhale makes us humans and animals healthier. Think about a "sick house" in the winter with closed up windows, no ventilation and the "sick building syndrome". This helps you avoid that, all for free.

There are dampers in my vents so that they are able to open and close to regulate air flow to and from the greenhouse.

You can make the process even more efficient by putting vents into the greenhouse from inside the home. This allows the solar fan to suck colder air from the home back into the greenhouse and then the fan takes the warmer, heated air from the greenhouse and blows that back into the home.

Vents on the greenhouse wall allow circulation of air between the home and the greenhouse.

On the back side of the vents in my home, I have similar vents in the greenhouse which I can open and close as well, as seen in the photo above.

You can reuse insulation from the wall to close up your fan at night.

In addition, I installed insect screen in the vents as well as on my fan that will keep insects from crawling from the greenhouse into my home through the vents or through the fan opening. In the summer time, I insulate the box with the fan, and then board it up until I need it again in the winter.

You can board up your solar fan when you are not using it.

Installing adjustable metal shelving will give you more storage and planting space.

At this point in the project you can install your metal adjustable wall shelving and then clean up any left-over construction debris so that you can get ready to begin growing plants in your greenhouse.

CHAPTER-9
A GROWING PLANTATION

I use sturdy adjustable metal shelving that was originally made for hanging clothes in closets for a number of things in my greenhouse. I use it to start plant seedlings, hold animal cages, and as trellises for climbing plant vines. The shelving can hold a lot of weight, is water proof, and can be adjusted to accommodate different size potted plants as they grow. I find the shelves were a worthwhile investment, as they give us much more growing area and allow us the flexibility to grow plants in 3 dimensions.

Metal shelving can allow you to grow plants in 3 dimensions.

Once you have established nitrogen fixing ground cover like clover in your plant beds, you can start planting seeds or seedlings in amongst the clover. We have grown everything in our greenhouse from "your garden variety vegetables" in the winter, to 6' tall corn stalks, to protect them from the raccoons, in the summer. We change the plants that we grow in the greenhouse based on their lifecycles and the seasons. For example, we grow greens in the late fall and winter, when those plants would not survive outside.

We start seedlings in pots or trays in the early spring so that any plants we put in the garden after the last spring frost, will be well established and healthy at the very start. This practice is a lot "safer" than planting your seeds in the ground of your garden too early in order to take full advantage of a short summer growing season. This is because, all too often, you can have a late spring frost, and after you have put plants in the ground, you can lose all those plants, before you see the "fruits of your labor".

You can start seeds in trays and then transplant them to small pots.

This is even more critical in a grid-down scenario, since if you plant all your seeds too early, and lose all your plants, you may be without food for an entire growing season. And if there are no more jobs or grocery stores, you can starve to death, from a late spring frost. Conversely, if you plant your seeds and seedlings too late in the season, they may not get to maturity in time to bear fruit before an early fall frost, again, leading to starvation of you and your family.

We usually start our annual vegetable seeds 6 – 8 weeks prior to the latest anticipated annual spring frost. This gives us the flexibility to plant seedlings in the garden when the weather is best and the plants are healthy and established. This also makes the plants stronger and less susceptible to early bug infestations that could otherwise destroy a young plant.

We plant non genetically modified (non GMO) heirloom seeds that "breed true" (they are what their parents were). Non GMO plants, are also able to be harvested for both food and for seeds, which we can replant again the following year.

Genetically modified organism (GMO) plants often produce seeds that are sterile and that will not reproduce new plants the following year. Likewise, hybrid plants may not produce the same fruit (or same quality fruit) in a second generation, so saving seeds from hybrids to replant in following years may not give you what you expect.

You can use the greenhouse to grow seedlings earlier in the season.

That is why we only grow heirloom plants and why we always save a small percentage of seeds from our harvest each season that allow us to grow new plants in successive years. This also allows us to have reliable crops year after year.

When starting your seedlings, you may want to mark your plants with popsicle sticks and/or tape on the pots, so that you know what is in each pot at outdoor planting time. It also allows you to see which seeds do well and which seeds do not, so that you can keep records for successive years. You obviously want to save the best seeds from your best plants, and keeping notes each year will help you to do that.

Beans, cucumbers, peanuts, passion fruit, mint, oats and comfrey growing together in a 2' x 2' space in the *Secret Garden of Survival*.

Although you can grow crops in the greenhouse plant beds in a number of ways, I encourage that you simply intermingle plants throughout your beds in amongst clover and other synergistic plants.

This method works better than traditional row planting, for the same reasons that I discuss in the ***Secret Garden of Survival- How to Grow a Camouflaged Food-Forest***. Plants do better together when they are allowed to intermingle, sharing resources and synergistic relationships, than they do in a "mono-crop" scenario where you are growing single crops in an area, and/or planting in rows.

Nature has grown plants this way for millions of years, long before man decided he would make things easier for himself to harvest, by planting all of the same crops in the same space, that all ripened at the same time.

This is not the way nature works. Nature prefers diversity.

You can use strings and a pipe to create guidelines for a square foot garden in your plant beds.

Of course, you can also grow plants in your beds using concepts like "square foot gardening". For those that wish to use this technique, you can easily create square foot garden beds by running nylon strings in one foot squares inside your beds. Since our planters are 2' wide in the **Secret Greenhouse of Survival,** you can string a line every foot (attached to a screw in the PVC trim) and split each string running across with another long string running the entire length of you planter bed, halfway down the center.

We tied our strings to screws in our PVC trim on the wall side of the greenhouse and attached the other end of each string to an empty ½" PVC pipe running along the inside cement wall. This makes it easy to slide, move, and adjust the strings to your needs.

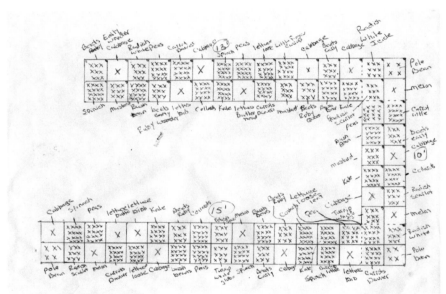

You can grow a tremendous amount of food using a square foot garden concept in your planters.

This gives you neat little 1' x 1' squares into which you can plant your square foot garden using your square foot garden plan.

Since your greenhouse planter beds are essentially a closed eco-system with no outside inputs, your growing plants can deplete nutrients from the soil over time. For many reasons that I outlined in my book **Secret Garden of Survival**, I don't believe in using commercial fertilizer. Instead, I use plants that add nitrogen and other nutrients back to the soil naturally. Aside from clover, other plants like edible mustard, beans, peas, peanuts and buckwheat can add nitrogen back to the soil.. You can also take advantage of recycling animal waste nutrients by using the straw bedding that comes out of your animal stalls and placing that in your planter beds. The straw also provides additional mulch for your plants.

"Used" straw from barn animal stalls provides mulch and nutrients.

Also, if you keep live animals in the greenhouse itself, (see Chapter 10) you can use their waste to fertilize your plants directly when your animal cages are placed on shelves over the planters. Likewise, straw bedding on the greenhouse floor where you may keep ducks or incubate other birds, can be used as a natural fertilizer in your greenhouse beds.

You can use shelves as trellises for climbing plants like peas.

7 ft. tall or longer vines can climb up shelving that can be used as trellises. Peas, beans, and other vining plants including cucumbers, and squash, can climb trellises and produce food off the ground. As odd as it may seem, squash and cucumbers do just fine by letting them grow up a trellis instead of running along the ground. Not only does this give them more air circulation, it also gives you a way to maximize growing space in your 2 ft. wide planter beds by growing in 3 dimensions.

In fact, allowing these plants to grow up in the air, makes them less apt to have bad bug problems while the good bugs hibernate during the winter. See the Bonus Chapter 12 at the end of this book for more information on controlling greenhouse pests without using chemical pesticides.

You can grow peas and greens for fresh salads in the winter time.

In the summer time, you can grow just about anything in the greenhouse and you can open windows and screens to let in pollinators like honeybees to pollinate your greenhouse crops. You can grow many of the same plants in the winter, however, you will have to manually pollinate these flowering plants with a Q-Tip swab.

Radishes, turnips, lettuce, spinach, collards, cabbage, beets, mustard and kale don't need pollination to produce food in the greenhouse.

Greens and many root crops, on the other hand, don't typically need to be pollinated since you eat the leaves(or roots) instead of the fruit or seeds. Therefore these greens and root crops can be grown in the winter months inside the greenhouse when no pollinators are available.

Many greens also will grow better in less intense sun and cooler temperatures of the winter greenhouse (since most greens don't do well in extreme mid-summer heat). So greens are uniquely suited for growth in the winter greenhouse.

Exotic trees can be moved into the greenhouse in cold temperatures.

If you live in a climate that has cold winters, you may be able to grow exotic plants such as coffee trees and citrus fruit in pots outdoors on your property during the summer, but you must move these plants inside during the winter. Your greenhouse is an excellent facility to house and grow exotic plants during colder months, while protecting them from the severe elements.

Citrus trees in pots can be moved into the greenhouse for the winter.

Citrus including lemons, oranges, grapefruit, limes, etc. can add vitamin C to a homesteader's diet and prevent scurvy, making you healthier overall.

This is especially important if we experience an "end of the world as we know it" scenario since you would not be able to buy fruit like this, when there are no grocery stores and no way to ship them from sub- tropical climates to wherever you may be located.

You can grow citrus outside in the summer time in pots, and then move those plants into your greenhouse before it gets too cold for them. During the summer, you can let pollinators like honey bees pollinate the citrus flowers and they will bear fruit. In the winter, when honey bees are not flying, you can pollinate the flowers yourself using a Q-Tip or other cotton swab.

By simply swabbing a number of flowers with the same Q-Tip, you will be spreading the pollen to the other flowers as you go, just as honey bees do. Remember, you must manually pollinate these plants, or they will flower in the greenhouse, and although the flowers may smell very sweet, they will never produce fruit, without your help in pollination.

You can also grow other exotic plants in your greenhouse like pomegranate, mangoes, and bananas in the same way. These special treats will be a welcome change from hum-drum vegetables, in a grid down situation. They also could be priceless as barter items in an end of the world as we know it scenario.

Coffee trees and coffee beans could be a rare commodity in the future.

Likewise, coffee trees and coffee beans could be a rare and valuable commodity in the future, since Juan Valdez probably won't be bringing coffee beans to your neck of the woods with his donkey after the end of the world as we know it.

As your exotic trees grow, you can transplant them to larger and larger pots, and as they grow, you can change their location from sitting on the sides of you planter walls to sitting on your greenhouse floor.

This is why, when planning your building, you want make sure that you have adequate floor space for plants and for you to be able to move around.

Taller plants like citrus trees can sit on the floor or on the planters.

You can grow new plants from old, like celery or Okinawa Spinach.

Many plants are easily propagated from existing stalks, roots, or cuttings, if you know how. For example, you can take a celery stalk after you have eaten the "good parts" and you can immerse the celery in a plastic cup filled with water in the greenhouse. The celery stalk will regenerate and you can eat if again!

Likewise, you can propagate Okinawa Spinach (which is rich in nutrients) by taking a cutting of a small branch, placing it in dirt or water, and thereby create an entirely new plant from that one cutting.

The greenhouse is an ideal, protected environment for these propagation activities.

You can also use your greenhouse to grow oats, wheat, barley and other "grasses" year round in your greenhouse, that produce grains for use in making cereals, bread, and beer, or for simply feeding the leaves (or grains) to your livestock.

Remember, there is a lot you can do with raw flour to make all kinds of foods, but if you don't have a renewable supply of these grains from which you can make flour, once you run out of the flour that is stored in your pantry, you may be out of it forever.

Edible raw or cooked, hardy Okinawa Spinach can be propagated from cuttings in the greenhouse.

Now that we have shown you how to grow plants in the *Secret Greenhouse of Survival,* let's look at how you can use your greenhouse to grow animal proteins that you can consume for a balanced diet.

CHAPTER-10
ANIMAL HOUSE

As I mentioned in my book *Secret Garden of Survival-How to Grow a Camouflaged Food-Forest*, studies of native indigenous people who lived off the land for thousands of years without modern conveniences, showed that they were able to survive by eating perennial fruits and nuts, as well as small animal proteins (birds, rabbits, fish, etc.)

You can use your greenhouse to raise animals and incubate birds.

Well, you can also use your *Secret Greenhouse of Survival* to raise a multitude of animals in the same space that you are growing plants.

You can raise chickens, ducks, and other birds in your greenhouse.

For example, since your greenhouse is a highly energy efficient building, you can use it to incubate chickens, ducks, guinea fowl, and turkeys until such time as they get old enough to be released into your garden. The young birds will be warm and safe on the floor of your greenhouse and you can partition off their incubation area, with movable cement blocks or boards, so that they do not interfere with your greenhouse plants. As they get older, you can expand their area as needed.

In fact, I had 15 full sized adult Khaki Campbell ducks in my greenhouse at one time, and they even had a series of nesting boxes on the greenhouse floor that I made with cement blocks and a board over the top, so that they could lay eggs in the greenhouse. Every morning I would pick up the eggs and let the ducks out into the garden, and every evening they marched back into the safety of their greenhouse for the night.

These ducks had a feed and water supply in the greenhouse and I simply threw straw on the floor so that I could clean up after them every other day or so. I took the nutrient rich straw and used it on the garden as mulch containing "fertilizer". Nothing went to waste, and they produced protein for me (both eggs and meat) and I did not have to build a special building or enclosure for them to do so.

Using your **Secret Greenhouse of Survival** to grow food and to house animals can be an ideal solution if you live in a neighborhood with restrictive covenants and a home owners association that will not allow you to build a barn, chicken coop, or otherwise have "farm" animals on your property. With the **Secret Greenhouse of Survival**, your neighbors would never know.

You can also grow rabbits in your greenhouse for protein and pelts.

Likewise you can grow rabbits securely in your **Secret Greenhouse of Survival**. Having rabbit hutches outdoors can be detrimental for you in a number of ways. First of all, predators such as raccoons have been known to kill livestock such as chickens and rabbits by grabbing them through the chicken wire with their claws, biting their heads off and then pulling them through the wire, piece by piece.

Aside from predators, your rabbits are also better protected from the elements in the controlled environment of your greenhouse. And in a grid down situation, your rabbits won't be a visually tempting meal for hungry passersby.

The rabbits also can fertilize your plants by your simply leaving the collection tray off the bottom of your rabbit cages, and allowing the rabbits to do what comes naturally over the plant beds in your greenhouse. By having your rabbits in the greenhouse on shelves, it is easier for you to care for them as well, since you do not have to go outside to feed them or clean their cages on rainy or freezing cold days.

Use aquaponics to grow food (fish and plants) in your greenhouse.

You can also grow fish in your greenhouse in either a complex or simple aquaponics system. In an aquaponics system, the fish tank water is recirculated to a tank containing plants. The plants feed off the nutrients in the fish water. The plants then clean up the water, so that the cleaned and fresh water can be returned to the fish.

Having an aquaponics system in your greenhouse allows you to grow fish year round, and allows you to do so discretely, so that neither your HOA, your neighbors, or any horde of zombies, will know you are growing fish on your property.

CHAPTER- 11
MADE IN THE SHADE CLOTH

Greenhouses can get hot. And even with open windows and solar fans running, sometimes the heat can be too intense during the summer months for growing plants and for livestock in the greenhouse. One typical solution for an overly hot greenhouse, is installing a shade cloth on the roof.

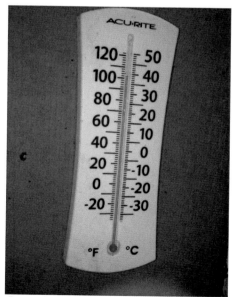

Greenhouses can get too hot for plants, animals and you.

Shade cloth can be ordered to fit the exact size of your greenhouse roof and comes with grommets so that you can secure the shade cloth onto your greenhouse, and so that it will not fly off in the wind or in other bad weather.

Shade cloth can also come in a number of densities, which allows you to have lighter or darker shades, depending on your area of the country, as well as the length and intensity of your summers.

With a shade cloth and proper ventilation, you can continue to grow vegetables like spinach, that are normally harvested before the intense heat and sun of summer.

Shade cloth and bungee cords to hold your shade cloth in place.

Once you have your shade cloth, you will need bungee cords to hold the grommets in the shade cloth onto eyebolts under the soffit of your greenhouse. (When you install the eyebolts make sure their position lines up with the grommets on your shade cloth).

Spread your shade cloth in front of the building and line up the grommets with eyebolts in the soffit up above.

Roll out your folded shade cloth in front of the building and line up the grommets so they match up with your eyebolts up above. Position ladders on either side of the greenhouse and have a helper to get the shade cloth lifted up onto the greenhouse roof.

Thread the loop of the bungee through the eyebolt and the grommet.

Once the shade cloth is on the roof, start with a corner and thread the looped end of the bungee through the eyebolt and then thread it through the corner grommet.

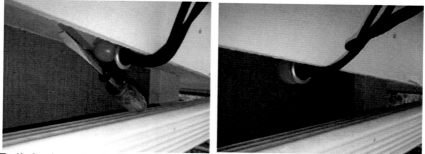

Pull the loop back through the eyebolt and over the ball.

Pull the looped end back down through the other side of the eyebolt and if necessary, use a screwdriver to pry the loop over the ball. Now pull the loop back through the eyebolt again toward the grommet.

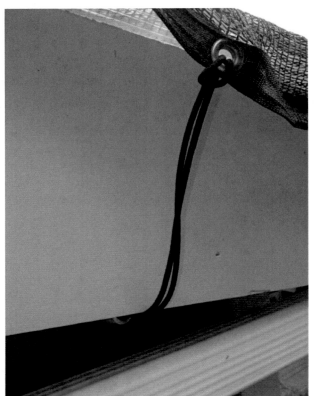

The result creates a "noose" around the grommet.

This will create a "noose" around the grommet and will hold it in place just over the eyebolt, but it will also allow it enough slack and stretch to "give" with the wind as well as expansion and contraction from hot and cold weather. The ball will not go through the eyebolt so your shade cloth is secure.

Repeat these steps for grommets all the way around the greenhouse.

Now continue and repeat with each eyebolt and each grommet until the shade cloth is secure all the way around the greenhouse.

You can cover the gutter with the shade cloth to keep out debris.

Since the shade cloth is porous and allows water to run through it, you can run your shade cloth over the gutters of your greenhouse to keep out debris. Water will still run into the gutter from the roof through the shade cloth, but leaves, sticks and other debris will not.

This "filtering" of debris can be helpful with your rain water collection in that significantly less organic material will get into your rainwater tank to foul your water with decaying matter.

Once the shade cloth is in place check all seams and connections to insure that the entire shade cloth is lined up and installed properly. Watch carefully during the next windy day to make certain that the shade cloth is not too loose and does not become a "sail" on top of your greenhouse. If it does, get shorter bungees or find a way to shorten them with knots.

Once finished, the shade cloth should be straight, square and relatively tight to the roof of the greenhouse.

When finished the shade cloth should be square and fairly tight.

Check the interior of the greenhouse and notice how much the cloth reduces the intense heat from before. Watch the temperature for a few days and notice how much more comfortable the greenhouse is for you and your plants.

The temperature in the greenhouse can drop as much as 20 degrees F once the shade cloth is installed.

Then come fall, when you have less intense days of sun, you can reverse the process and take off the shade cloth, and roll it up for next year.

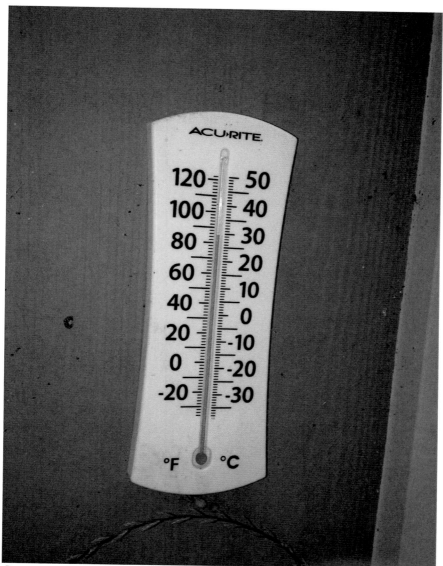

Our greenhouse temperature went from over 105 degrees down to 85 degrees within minutes after installing the shade cloth.

BONUS CHAPTER-12
PEST CONTROL

Mountain mint attracts predatory wasps that kill bad garden bugs.

In the *Secret Garden of Survival*, I use natural pest control so that I do not have to use chemical pesticides. First of all, chemical pesticides invariably end up in the food you eat. Secondly, chemical pesticides will also kill the beneficial microorganisms in your plant beds. If you kill those beneficial microorganisms, they cannot release critical nutrients into the soil that your plants will need to grow properly.

So in the *Secret Garden of Survival* one pest control method that I use, is to attract predatory wasps with plants like Mountain Mint. Those predatory wasps that feed on the mint nectar, will also prey on and kill the bad bugs that you don't want on your other garden plants.

Unfortunately, you don't necessarily have the opportunity to use predatory wasps in a greenhouse with closed doors, windows and screens.

Although you can certainly open your windows and screens in the summer to let predatory insects into the greenhouse to naturally take care of greenhouse pests, in the winter time, those flying predators are not available since they are all hibernating while it is cold. Therefore, you need to have other options that are natural forms of pest control which would be alternatives to using poison chemicals on the food that you eat.

Spider egg sacks in your greenhouse can save your crops.

Maybe you are freaked out by spiders. But if you want to grow food, you shouldn't be. In fact, you should learn to love spiders. I don't mean that you should become a spider lover or collector. I just mean that you need to learn to appreciate what they do-*for you*. Understand this one fact: Nothing eats as many garden pests as spiders do. In fact, spiders are the most numerous land predators on the planet. And for gardeners, that's a good thing.

To put spiders to work for you, you just need to create a habitat that appeals to spiders, so they will protect your crops from pests that feed on your plants.

Weeds are good for your garden plants and as habitats for good bugs.

For those that have read my book, *Secret Garden of Survival*, you know that I say "weeds are good". Weeds are nature's pioneer plants and they help establish garden soil so that other plants can grow successfully.

Now here is another reason that weeds are good. If you have carefully weeded your garden and have bare ground between your plants, chances are that you've created a habitat that will attract a lot of harmful insects and very few, if any, spiders to eat them. Since spiders need shade and protection from their own predators (like birds, etc.) weeds give spiders the "cover and concealment" needed so that they can do their jobs in your garden. Plus having weeds between your plants gives web building spiders a place to make their webs, near the plants that you want to protect.

Finished Frame With Decomposed Mulch in the Foreground.

As you have probably figured out by now, I am also an advocate of using good decomposed mulch in your garden. Aside from bringing in good micro-organisms, and helping to retain moisture in the soil and reducing watering needs, a loose layer of mulch also creates a great habitat for hunting spiders where they can hide and stay cool, while they wait to ambush the bad bugs you don't want eating in your garden. So just like in your garden, maintain a good layer of mulch on top of your greenhouse plants beds.

Thus, if you are lucky enough to get spiders in your greenhouse, keep them around and on your payroll. If you don't have spiders in your greenhouse, you can easily collect spider egg sacks and relocate them into your greenhouse, so that they will hatch in the warm environment, and go to work for you.

Just like spiders prey on insects, so do salamanders, lizards and skinks. Again, maybe they freak you out, but they should not. They are part of nature's system of pest control that will protect your garden plants, and they can do well in a warm greenhouse environment.

A toad may not be a prince in disguise, but he sure can eat a lot of bugs. In one night a toad can eat 100 army worms, cutworms, snails, slugs tent caterpillars or sow bugs. Toads are great to have in your garden, and you can also have them in your greenhouse, but they would need a moist environment, a place to escape the heat (you can make a tunnel in you beds with another PVC pipe) and a source of water.

You can eliminate ants by letting them eat corn meal.

Ants can be a problem in your raised beds and in your greenhouse pots; particularly if you move pots in from outdoors, which you may do during inclement weather.

Although ants have their purpose in nature, you don't want to be dealing with ants in your raised beds, particularly if they are fire ants.

One non poison solution to getting rid of ant colonies is to spread cornmeal around the mound or where the ants seem to be congregating. The ants bring the cornmeal back into the colony and the ants eat it. Unfortunately (for them) the corn meal absorbs water and expands in their stomachs, basically exploding the ant. As long as they have fed the queen(s) in the colony (as would be proper royal ant etiquette), you can eliminate the whole colony.

Another non-lethal option (for you) is to pour boiling water right into and onto the colony mound. This will scald the ants, but it may also scald your plant rootss, so depending upon what you have planted and how badly you want to get rid of the ants, use the boiling water method accordingly.

Baby chicks can rid you of bugs and also fertilize your beds.

You can also place chickens or baby chicks in the planter beds. They will eat bugs in your beds and will also drop their natural fertilizer as they go. Again, be careful with what you have planted, as chickens, particularly the large ones, can do more harm than good if they scratch up your plant roots.

Mice can be another problem in your greenhouse. Just as your plants like a warm and protected environment in the winter, so do mice. Try as you might to keep them out, they can find a way in. Using poison traps may not be the best idea because poison could spread into your beds and be taken up by your plant roots, or the mice could die in the wall or behind a planter. You don't want to be smelling that- especially if you are taking heated air from the greenhouse in the winter and using that to heat your home.

There really is a better mousetrap out there.

In order to eliminate mice, a good old mouse trap is usually your best option. The only bait you need for mouse traps is a little peanut butter.

There is an old adage that says "build a better mouse trap and the world will beat a path to your door". Well, from my experience, there are certainly better mousetraps today than others.

Wooden ones can snap on your fingers, and are prone to break (the staple pulls out of spring and then it is useless). And although the simplest wooden traps are cheaper, you may find yourself replacing them too often. And some of the wooden traps just don't release when they should, so the mice can eat the peanut butter without setting the trap. (There is nothing worse than going out in the morning to find the peanut butter eaten out and trap, but it was not set.)

On the other hand, the mouse trap on the left in the picture above is the best trap I have used. Peanut butter is placed in a tray under the black cover with just enough space for mouse nose to sniff. The mouse cannot get at the peanut butter without sticking his nose in the trap, and he can only do that from the front- so he can't eat the food out of the tray and not get snapped. And as soon as he sticks his little nose in to eat, the black cover lifts up, which sets off the guillotine arm of the trap to smack down and break the mouse's neck. Quick, painless, and effective.

And another benefit is that since it happens so fast, that the mouse and his friends don't get to eat the peanut butter out of the trap- so when you walk back in, you just take out the deceased mouse and reset the trap – without having to put new peanut butter in the trap. And thus, you don't have to waste more peanut butter on catching pests. (Which could be important since peanut butter would be a valuable commodity that you will need for your own survival food, in a grid-down situation).

Aphids are another greenhouse pest that can become a problem if left unchecked.

Aphids are tiny soft bodied insects that at first glance don't look like they can do much harm, but they multiply fast and before you know it, the underside or your leaves could be covered as they collectively suck the juice out of your plants. Outdoors, aphids have natural predators that keep them in check, but since your greenhouse is a closed system, and since their predators are mostly hibernating for the winter, you could lose your indoor crops in short order unless you find a way to get rid of them.

In the field, ladybugs are one of the best natural controls for aphids. The ladybugs (and their off spring) feed on the aphids, thus eliminating your problem. In the late fall you may notice that ladybugs are looking for places to stay over the winter. If you "invite them in" to your greenhouse, you can have them as seasonal guests that will earn their keep by eating the aphids.

Aphids are tiny bugs, but will suck the juice out of plant leaves.

If you have not been lucky enough to have lady bugs come to visit inside your greenhouse, you can also take care of your aphid problem with a little concoction that you can make from dried tomato leaves.

We all know that we should harvest our tomatoes out of our garden, but what do you do with the green tomato plants after the season is over?

Well you can harvest the leaves and dry them in a paper bag and store the bag in a cool dry place (like your pantry). Then if you start to notice aphids on your greenhouse plants, you can make a tea that will take care of the problem.

You can harvest tomato leaves to make a spray that will kill aphids.

To make the tea, bring 2 cups of water to a boil. Then take a cup of the leaves and add them to the boiling water. Remove the pan from the heat, and let it steep overnight.

In the morning you can discard the leaf parts and then pour the "tomato leaf tea" into a used (and clean) spray bottle. Then just spray the tea on your infested leaves. Be sure to spray under the leaves where the aphids hide, to get the maximum effect.

The tea contains alkaloids from the tomato plant, and although the tea won't harm your plants, it will kill the soft bodied aphids.

Use a spray bottle to feed a tomato "tea" to your unwanted guests.

Although this is a book on how to build the *Secret Greenhouse of Survival*, many of these non-chemical, and more natural, pest control remedies can be used elsewhere in your home or garden.

Many of them could be invaluable, especially if we have a situation, where chemical options, sprays and poisons are not available or non-existent.

Of course it is my contention that you should not, and do not need to be using chemical options in the first place.

(I'VE COME TO A)
CONCLUSION

Imagine a greenhouse that heats your home in the winter; heats your water; grows 5x more food per sq. ft. than a hoop house; provides food for your family all year long; grows exotic foods (i.e. citrus in New England); starts seedlings in spring; hides your solar electric system; can house your small animals and incubate chickens and ducks.   All disguised to look like a porch on your home.

This greenhouse does all that.

The Secret Greenhouse of Survival does all of the above.

It has been my hope that you have learned not only how to build your own *Secret Greenhouse of Survival*, but that you have also learned many tips and tricks that you can use for your own sustainable homesteading, building, and gardening.

Follow the instructions for your own greenhouse, as I have outlined them here. Keep me posted on your success. Send me questions, pictures and let me (and others on my website) experience how you are doing.

Sign up for my newsletter at www.SecretGardenOfSurvival.com which will provide you with free tips and tricks, as well as prepper and homesteading news and ideas. Ask me questions. I will answer them individually or on the website…

If you haven't done so already, pick up my book the *Secret Garden of Survival- How to Grow a Camouflaged Food-Forest*, and find out how you can create a survival food garden that provides all the fruit, veggies, nuts and berries that you and your family can consume, that you will only have to plant it once, where you never have to use fertilizer or use pesticide, and where you can harvest your food for a lifetime, all disguised so that no one else would know you have food growing there.

Now you know how to create your own *Secret Greenhouse of Survival*.

This greenhouse will help you to survive after your food stores run out and it will disguise your greenhouse garden and your food from the hordes from who would otherwise consume it after the fit hits the shan.

You will have an indoor survival food garden that provides all the fruit, veggies, leafy greens and citrus fruit that you and your family can consume, with 3-4 plantings per year, and a place to grow your animals, under cover and without anyone else noticing.

Good luck with your own *Secret Greenhouse of Survival* and be looking at our website, newsletter, and twitter feeds for tips on how to do even more with your new "indoor" food forest.

-The Survivalist Gardener

The End(s)

APPENDIX
MAKING A PLAN

Now that you have been through the whole book, you have seen the photos and followed along with each step and the reasoning for it. To take the next step to construct your own *Secret Greenhouse of Survival*, you need to create a master plan for the building process. Then you can figure out what you can do yourself, or what you need to hire others to do for you.

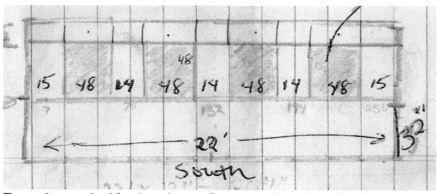

Draw the south side elevation to figure out lengths and heights.

You don't have to be an architect. You just have to be able to do some basic sketching (like the ones that I did here) that can outline your plan. And by doing this, you will have a much better feel for how the project needs to be done, so you can either do all of it yourself, or so that you can explain it to others that you may enlist to help you.

How to figure the Dimensions

The first thing you should determine will be the length of your *Secret Greenhouse of Survival*. (See the illustration above.)

For maximum effect you can make the greenhouse just slightly shorter than the full length of the south side of your home. By maximizing the size of the south side of your greenhouse you will maximize your solar gain.

Of course you can always make the building smaller; but the incremental additional cost saved by shaving off a few feet is minimal, compared to the costs for everything else. And the incremental cost of each additional foot of length is cheap compared to the benefits that each additional linear foot can give you in food production and energy gain.

In our drawing above, we figured that since our home was 24' on the south side, we should have a 22' greenhouse building in front of it. And since each course of concrete block for the foundation walls is 8" tall, we determined that our wall should be 32" off the ground or 4 courses (8" x 4 = 32") tall. This allows for enough height for the planters, and keeps the windows off the ground to avoid getting kicked and broken, as well as being above the snow level in the winter time.

To maximize glazing, we determined that we could have 4' (48") wide windows and that would allow us adequate room to put framing around those windows (to hold them in place) of 15"-14" on each side of each window.

(Note: You can determine the actual frame size needed to frame the rough the opening for each window from the manufacturer's specifications - which you can usually get off the side of the windows when you are shopping for windows at your window retailer.)

We also wanted enough ceiling height in the front (south side) of the building and so with an adequate header to hold the windows and roof in place, we determined that our windows could also be 4' (48") tall. So we are able to put standard 48" x 48" sliding windows in the front of the building.

We were able to ascertain all of the above, from that simple drawing on the first page of this Appendix. All you have to do is put pencil to paper, have a good ruler, and a calculator, and you can figure all this out too.

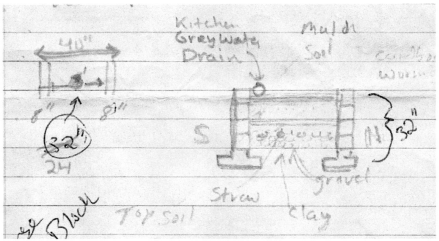

The width of your cinder block planters can help to determine the overall building width.

Next we need to determine the best width for the building which we can do by first determining the inside dimensions needed for the greenhouse. The greenhouse obviously needs to be wide enough so that you can work comfortably with your planting and plant care activities.

To determine the room you can work in, you should first determine the size of your planter beds. I suggest that you want your beds to be no smaller than a 2 ft. inside diameter so that you can have plenty of plants growing there and you probably want them no larger than a 3 ft. inside diameter, as anything wider would be very difficult for the average person to reach.

Let's assume that we use a size that is 2 ft.' inside. If we take 8" wide cement block walls on each side of the planter and add 2 ft. (24") to that, this would make the planter (8" + 8" + 24" = 40") or 3.3ft. wide. (See the illustration above- top left corner.)

So having two planters on each side of the greenhouse would take up 6.6' of space in the width of your building, just for the planters and block work.

So approximately 7 ft.' of planters plus 5 ft. of work space for you to walk around in would be a 12 ft. wide greenhouse. Obviously you can make the greenhouse wider if you want wider planters, but be careful not to make the planters too wide or you won't be able to reach the plants inside the planters.

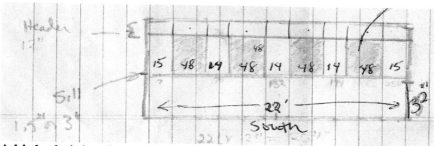

Add the height of your blocks, windows and header to determine the height off the ground of your building and roof.

I figured I would need 12" of space for the window headers and boards tying them together. I also knew that I would need a sill plate on top of the concrete to hold the frame to the concrete of 1 ½" (a standard 2" x 6" wood frame) plus another 1 ½" for the frame.

So, given the height of the windows being 48" and the height of the windows off the ground being at least 32" (for 4 courses of block) and add that to a 12" tall header and 3" frame to hold it all together- my south (front) roof was going to be 8 ft. tall. (48" + 32" + 12" + 3" = 95") Since 96" = 8 ft., our roof would be pretty close to 8ft. tall in the front (south side).

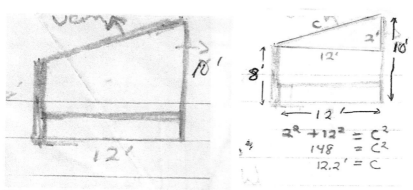

You can figure the building height and roof length using geometry.

The height of your back (north) greenhouse roof probably can't be higher than the windows on your second floor, if you want to use those windows all year long. Plus if you create a two story greenhouse, it will defeat the purpose of trying to make the building inconspicuous.

On the back side of the greenhouse (touching the house) in order to fit under my 2nd floor house windows, the back roof needed to be about 10' off the ground. Keep in mind that you will also need a sloped roof in order for rain and snow to slide off your greenhouse roof, so you do not want it to be flat.

Therefore, after I determined that my front (south side) greenhouse roof was going to be 8 ft. tall, and my back (north side) roof could be 10 ft. tall, I needed to determine the length of my roof.

Once you know the height off the ground of your front and back roof, you can figure the roof length (from front to back) by using simple geometry to solve for the longest leg (hypotenuse) of a triangle. Using the formula $a^2 + b^2 = c^2$, the roof would be 12.2 ft. long. (See the red pen triangle in the illustration above and to the right.)

But since I needed an overhang on both sides and the front, (so that water won't run down the sides of the greenhouse and so that I can collect rainwater on the low/south side for rain water collection), I added a little less than foot to the length of the roof, so it would be long enough to go past a soffit and into a gutter. That gave me a roof of about 13 ft. in length.

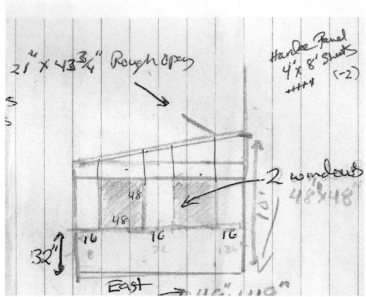

Determine the size, number, and location of your east side windows.

Now that you have determined that the sides of the building are to be 12 ft. wide, you can determine the size of the windows for your building sides.

As you can see from the measurements in the illustration above, the width of the windows on the east side of the building could again be the standard 48" x 48" sliding windows to maximize the glazing and to provide enough internal wood framing to allow for stability of the entire wall and the frame between each window. (In this case there was 16"of framing between each window.)

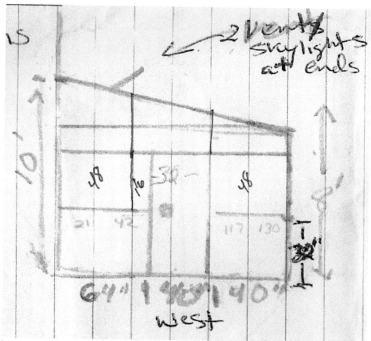

You will need a door between your blocks to get in and out.

On the west side, we needed to allow for a door to get in and out of the greenhouse. We decided not to include any windows on this side as we needed wall space for tools, for shelving and for a solar exhaust fan. We also determined that we could allow light in during the late afternoon on the west side of the building by having a screen door.

When planning, make sure that you leave a hole in the concrete block and wood framing wide enough for a door to get plants in and out from your garden. To determine the size of the concrete block opening for the door frame, you can find out the size of the door frame's necessary rough opening, from the manufacturer's specifications.

We also planned for additional door framing material so that we could eventually put in a security screen door that would bolt to that frame. As discussed in Chapter 6, the security screen door allowed us to leave the metal exterior door open on hot days or on hot nights and still keep unwanted pests such as bugs, rodents, raccoons, and humans out of the greenhouse.

Roof Plan

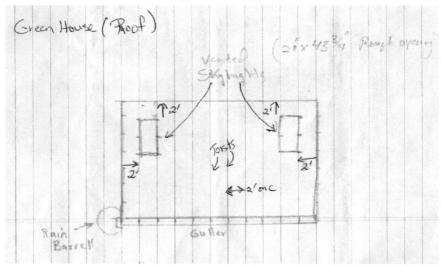

You will also need a plan for the framing of your roof and skylights.

To support the ceiling, we used 2" x 10" joists running from the front to the back of the greenhouse. In our plan, and we had a joist every 2ft on center. (During our actual build, our framing crew thought it better if we made it stronger by using framing at 16" on center.)

We also planned for a gutter on the south (low front) side. This gutter would be connected to a rain barrel for rain water collection.

Another important aspect to plan for is the framing for vented skylights to relieve high heat at the top of the greenhouse during hot days. With vented skylights you can open your vents as needed. You can find the sizes for the frame rough opening for your skylights windows from the manufacturer of the vented skylights that you choose.

Concrete Planning

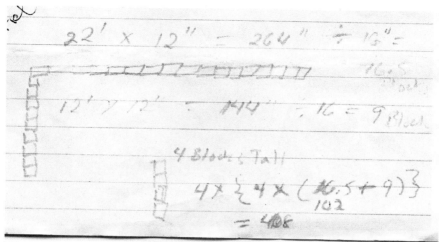

How to figure how many blocks you need.

A typical concrete block is 8" tall x 8" wide x 16" long. You will need to figure out how many blocks at 16" long it will take to reach the length of your building.

So with our 22 ft. front side wall, you can figure the length in inches (22 ft. x 12" to the foot) to give you 264". Divide that by 16" per block and you get 16.5 (or 16 ½) cinder blocks for one course on that side.

Then you need to multiply that by the number of the number of blocks stacked in your wall. In our case we stacked our blocks 4 blocks high. Since the blocks are each 8" high, our total wall would be 32" high.

Now if you multiply the number of blocks long, by the number of blocks stacked up (16.5 x 4), you can determine that you need 66 blocks for that one wall.

Of course, you need to have a parallel course of block on the inside of the greenhouse so that you can have 2 ft. wide planters. Once you figure the lengths (in inches) you can divide that number by 16" and that will give you the approximate the number of concrete blocks you will need per course. Then multiply that number by 4 (for 4 courses tall) and you will have the total number of concrete blocks.

You can figure the sides using the same formula.

Of course you need to deduct the blocks from the exterior door and the interior door (from inside the greenhouse into your home). That way you can leave a hole in the blocks where the door frames are going to go.

In my case, I figured that I would need a total of 408 concrete blocks to do the job. Make sure you order more than you need, because some will break, or you may need to cut some blocks to get around corners, etc.

Foundation/ Footing

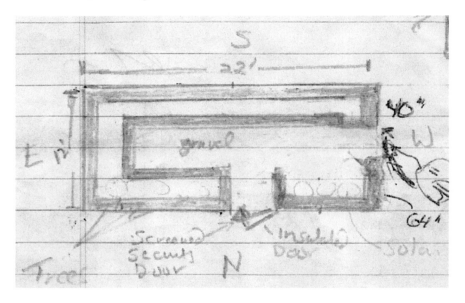

To support where your concrete block will be laid, you will need a "footer" of poured concrete with rebar running throughout. Your footers should be at least 12" wide (mine were 16") and 12" deep on which to lay your concrete block. You will also want to leave an opening (no concrete poured) in what will be the bottom of each planter, so that water can drain back to the ground inside the planters.

I also suggest that you do not want to have a concrete floor in your greenhouse. This is because you will be using a lot of water in your greenhouse and you will need it to drain without having to constantly mop it up from a concrete floor. Instead, we filled up the floor space with crushed rock for drainage, which keeps the floor from becoming a mud bath. The rock also added to the thermal mass of the greenhouse. (I recommend that you use 4- 6" of crushed stone for your floor.)

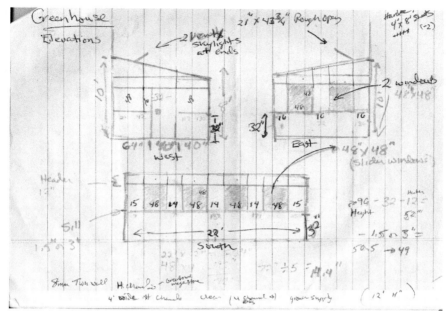

You can figure what you need for siding by adding up the space between windows.

You will also need to figure what you will need for siding in order to fill in between the windows, around the doors, etc.

I used cement board siding both outside and inside the building because it is durable and because it is made out of cement- so it won't rot or warp like wood in a high humidity environment. And being cement, it also adds to your thermal mass.

Costs:

Once you have figured out the dimensions you need to make a list of the materials that you will need as well as the costs of those materials.

If you are not handy, or lack time, you will need to factor in labor to do the block work and framing. The job is not complex, but if you are not a "do-it-yourselfer" you may want to hire people with experience to do it for you. I suggest that you can share this book and the diagrams with them, so that they will understand what you are trying to achieve with this project.

Of course, anything you do needs to meet your local building codes, so make sure you have a conversation with a licensed contractor and/or your local building inspector so that you will know what you need to do to meet the building requirements. Remember, this is a greenhouse, so there are often far less restrictions or inspection requirements (if any at all) for a greenhouse building. Just check with your local ordinances.

One other point to consider is that the block work in particular can be less expensive if you have a local professional install it for you. I found that the masons I hired could do the work in less than one day, and the cost of them to do it (including the materials), was cheaper than I could buy just the materials for alone.

If you have not done so already, read through the rest of this book and you will have a better understanding of what you will need for materials, once you see it all together.

Good luck and keep my posted on how you do!

CONTACT!
INFORMATION

Survivalist Gardener Web Links:

Website: www.SecretGardenofSurvival.com

Facebook: www.facebook.com/SecretGardenOfSurvival

Twitter: www.twitter.com/SurvivorGarden   (@SurvivorGarden)

Google+: Survivalist Gardner

Linkedin: www.linkedin.com/in/survivalistgardener

YouTube: http://www.youtube.com/survivalistgardener

Pintrest: www.pintrest.com/SurvivorGarden

Secrets of a Survivalist Radio Show:

http://www.preparednessradio.com/shows/secrets-of-a-survivalist-rick-austin/

ABOUT THE AUTHOR
(OK-SO IT IS ALL ABOUT ME.)

Rick Austin is known as the Survivalist Gardener, and is a preparedness and off grid living expert. He is the author of *Secret Garden of Survival-How to Grow a Camouflaged Food Forest* which is now the #1 Best Selling book in Garden Design.

Rick has also been featured on National Geographic Channel's *Doomsday Castle*, as well as the documentary film *Beyond Off Grid* and in *Mother Earth News*.

For more info and all his social media links, go to his website: www.SecretGardenOfSurvival.com

You can also hear Rick on his radio show *Secrets of a Survivalist* where each week he talks with the world's best survival experts that share their own secrets of survival.

http://www.preparednessradio.com/shows/secrets-of-a-survivalist-rick-austin/

Made in the USA
Columbia, SC
08 June 2022

61522200R00077